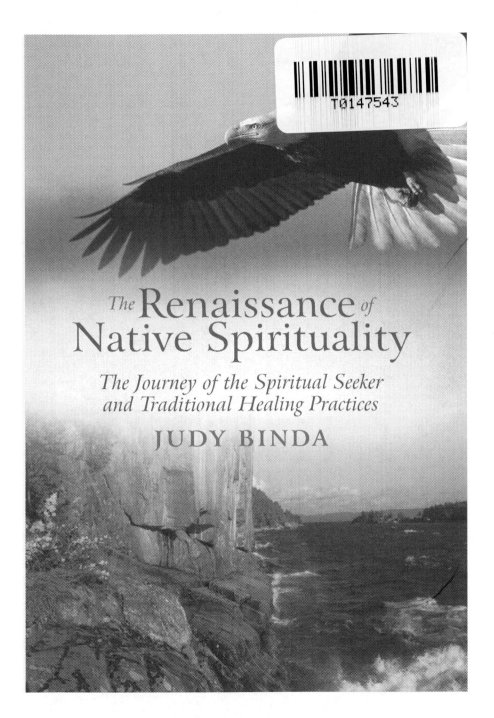

The Renaissance *of*
Native Spirituality

The Journey of the Spiritual Seeker
and Traditional Healing Practices

JUDY BINDA

iUniverse, Inc.
Bloomington

T0147543

The Renaissance of Native Spirituality
The Journey of the Spiritual Seeker and Traditional Healing Practices

Copyright © 2011 Judy Binda

All rights reserved. No part of this book may be used or reproduced by any means,
graphic, electronic, or mechanical, including photocopying, recording, taping or by any
information storage retrieval system without the written permission of the publisher
except in the case of brief quotations embodied in critical articles and reviews.

iUniverse books may be ordered through booksellers or by contacting:

iUniverse
1663 Liberty Drive
Bloomington, IN 47403
www.iuniverse.com
1-800-Authors (1-800-288-4677)

Because of the dynamic nature of the Internet, any Web addresses or links contained in
this book may have changed since publication and may no longer be valid. The views
expressed in this work are solely those of the author and do not necessarily reflect the
views of the publisher, and the publisher hereby disclaims any responsibility for them.

Any people depicted in stock imagery provided by Thinkstock are models,
and such images are being used for illustrative purposes only.

Certain stock imagery © Thinkstock.

ISBN: 978-1-4620-2782-8 (sc)
ISBN: 978-1-4620-2783-5 (hc)
ISBN: 978-1-4620-2784-2 (e)

Library of Congress Control Number: 2011909948

Printed in the United States of America

iUniverse rev. date: 6/27/2011

Contents

PART 1:
Native Spirituality

Acknowledgments

The following ethnographic research study on Native Spirituality is based on real life stories of Native American people talking about their spirituality. For the purpose of this study, real names are not used in order to protect their identities. I am grateful to the contributors, who seek to understand the Creator and creation and their spiritual journeys on Mother Earth. They have given unconditionally to benefit others.

Thank you to my professors from St. Cloud State University, Saint Cloud, Minnesota, where I conducted my Anthropology and American Indian studies.

I am grateful to my spiritual helpers who have crossed my path to help me heal, grow in spirit, and guide me as I have searched for the meaning of life on Mother Earth, including those who feel God's presence but do not realize fully God's ways. They have helped me to grow stronger and have taught me to believe more heartily in God, our Creator.

My journey has not been without trials and tribulations. I have faced negativity that has affected my humanness, overturned my life, and restricted my growth. There are many lessons we are here to learn in life. We will continue to repeat our journeys until we learn what we are here to learn and find our purpose in life. My spirit and spirit helpers are strong, which helps me to overcome my hardships. The Creator is always there, helping me to see beyond the norm of everyday existence, each step of the way. I pray for help, and help comes my way, as the power of God is stronger than any inhabitant of this earth or beyond our universe.

Believe in the higher power, for God shall prevail above all. He will carry you through as he carries your spirit over a threshold into an astonishing light beyond our physical world, to the point at which the very footprints of our humanness fade from Mother Earth and we leave as spiritual beings.

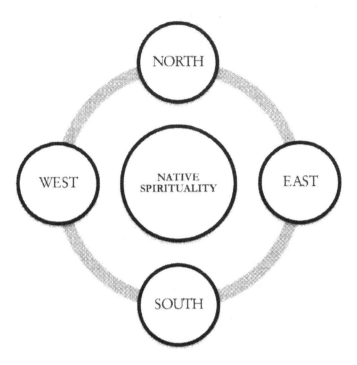

Native Spirituality

The Journey

of the

Spiritual Seeker

Introduction

I am an Anishinaabe woman following my traditional path, and I come from a family of twelve, with six females and six males. I was born and raised in Wawa, Ontario. I am the seventh sibling and I was raised Catholic by my parents and continue to believe in the higher power, God. My mother was Cecilia Margaret Binda (nee Belleau), who was an Ojibwe woman from the Garden River First Nation, Garden River, Ontario. She was born in 1925 and was an angelic and loving mother and grandmother. My father, Alcibiede Aldebrando Binda, was born in Padua, Italy in 1905 and immigrated to Canada in 1925. He was a loving and caring father, husband, and grandfather. They have both passed on into the spirit world, ending their journeys on Earth that the Creator had set out for them.

My own spiritual journey has brought me from Sault Ste. Marie, Ontario, Canada to St. Cloud State University in Saint Cloud, Minnesota, United States, to pursue a major in Anthropology and a minor in American Indian Studies. My study of anthropology has brought me to the point of writing this ethnography on Native Spirituality, based on ethnographic research with contributors from Minnesota, South Dakota, and Ontario. It is written for the Native people who understand their spiritual journeys as well as for those who are meant to find their traditional paths, for the spiritual seekers and the ethnographers who want to learn about Native spiritual ways.

I believe that there is a higher spiritual self within each human being, and that this spiritual self was sent to this earth by the Creator from a place outside of our physical world: the spirit world, where spirits dwell. The Creator put us on this human journey as spirits in human bodies, and we choose the life that we have, as we have chosen our parents. If you believe in your higher spiritual self, you will have a deeper understanding of your spiritual journey and your connection to the Creator. My Native spiritual journey commenced long before I was born, and through spiritual guidance it has brought me to an awakening of my mind, body, and spirit. I want to show you a path to an understanding of my own journey, as well as the journeys of my Native subjects, who gave of themselves unconditionally in participating in my

5

research study on Native Spirituality. I will start by telling you how it began for me, and how my Native study participants found their spiritual paths.

My spiritual journey began long before I was conceived. My infancy and childhood experience was not without meaning to my journey. My awareness of my spiritual journey started when I was in my twenties, when I had a spiritual experience. As I passed over into the spirit world, I had an out-of-body experience, which means that my spirit left my body. According to Betty J. Eadie, our physical bodies are like cocoons that embrace our spirits, and when we die, our bodies are left to return to the earth and our spirits journey on to the spirit world. Of course, after this experience, my spirit returned to my body. I saw, felt, and was aware of the spiritual journey; I had departed into a darkness and then into a miraculous brilliant light. It was my awakening; it was the time in my life when I became aware that my existence would be of importance to Native people in some way. I was taken away swiftly, and it seemed that only a short period of time passed. The day after my experience, all that I could recall was the message that I needed to learn about my Native culture. I started to replay the experience in my mind—what I had seen, and what had transpired. The experience stayed with me for a long time. I spent nearly two years trying to find out what had happened to me. I visited a local doctor to get checked physically for any health-related condition that may have induced my out-of-body experience. I also spoke to Native elders, asking them if they could tell me about this other place, the other dimension to which I had traveled.

I connected to an elder who was walking his spiritual path: Great White Eagle was from the Michipicoten First Nation, near where I was born. He has since passed on to the spirit world. I began to attend ceremonies at his home, and I took the first steps toward my journey. I was given my spirit name, clan, and colors. Another Native woman and I participated in a naming ceremony (see appendix) to acknowledge our spiritual significance as Anishinaabe women. The woman was named "Rainbow Woman" and is of the hummingbird clan. I carry the name of "White Eagle Woman," and my clan is Makwa, or Bear clan. My colors—white, light yellow, purple, light blue, and fuchsia—came to me spiritually. As the Great White Eagle man asked me to look up at Grandfather Sun, I did, and closed my eyes. Then the colors came to me one by one, as veils passing across the darkness of my eyelids. The experience was magical. I was in awe of what I saw: beautiful radiant colors, which were a reflection of me. My name was meaningful, my clan significant, and my colors radiant, proclaiming my recognition of who I was as an Anishinaabe. A door had opened.

In the course of my travels, seeking understanding of my spiritual experience, in 1998, I attended a women's gathering outside of Chapleau,

Ontario. It was the "Gathering of Women, Nurturing our Spirit" conference. There, I met Betty J. Eadie from South Dakota. She was the keynote speaker, and as she spoke about her spiritual experiences of passing over into the spirit world, once as a child and once as an adult woman, I connected with her words. Later, I got to talk with her personally, at which time I asked her deeper questions relating to my own experience. As I told her what had happened to me, she asked me if I was sure that I had really gone there. Yes, I said; I was in the light and had heard a voice call my name, "Judy," ever so softly. It was then that she told me that I would be helping women of different ages; I will share that journey on the following pages.

My journey later took me to meet another elder in Northern Ontario, the late Edith, a woman who carried the gift of seeing into people's lives and the gift of spirit travel. She held my hand and spoke in her language, Oji-Cree. She said, "The Creator has sent you here," as her son, "Indian Joe," translated her words into English. I did not understand totally what she meant at that moment. But as I left, flying over the small community on Bearskin Airlines, I shed tears and felt a connection to the people and place of this remote area in Northern Ontario. It is a place deep within the green forests and it brings peace and serenity. I carried the message that was given to me in my heart, knowing that I would understand one day why I ended up meeting Edith on my path.

I continued to seek out further knowledge about my experience through Native ceremonies. I was living in Wawa, Ontario in 1999, when I received a call from my brother who told me that a Shaky Tent ceremony and a Third Eye ceremony (see appendix) were being held at the Healing Lodge in Garden River, Ontario, about 238 km (148 miles) south of Wawa. I attended the Third Eye ceremony, which was conducted by the elder Theon. When I arrived, the ceremony was nearly over. I went up to the elder Theon, passed my gift of tobacco to him, and asked him if he could still do the ceremony for me. He agreed, saying, "I knew there was one more coming, as I could not pour out all the fish oil."

As he conducted the ceremony to open my third eye, I saw a light appear over my eyes. He later said to me, "You have been traveling and searching all over," and I responded, "Yes, I have." He told me that what I had been looking for was right here, that I did not have to go far to find it.

My search for my spirituality and connection was bearing fruit; I knew and felt that I had a deeper understanding of my journey. I had attended the Shaky Tent ceremony to find out more of what my journey would entail, and the elder Theon had said, "When you were over there in the spirit world, they told you things. They were women; you don't know yet, but it will come back to you when the time is right, what they said to you." This opened a new and different facet of understanding. I now had more knowledge about the event that had taken me to another dimension, the spirit world.

Years later, when I was attending St. Cloud State University in Minnesota, I decided to pursue my passion for Native spirituality in a more formal academic setting. I chose to conduct my research through anthropological research and research methods using qualitative semi-structured interviews with Native people in Minnesota, South Dakota, and Ontario, to provide a broader understanding of how individuals of different nations perceive their personal spiritual journeys. I conducted participant observations at a sun dance at Pipestone, Minnesota and the Milles Lacs reservation's big drum ceremony. Prior to my anthropological research, I attended many sweat lodges, shaky tents, cedar baths, talking circles, and powwows in Ontario before moving south to Minnesota. I traveled around the Milles Lacs reservation (three tribal areas) and Wisconsin attending big drum ceremonies with a local traditional woman, and I attended a sun dance at Pipestone. My spiritual journey to the spirit world and my physical journey on earth as a spirit having a human experience inspired me to conduct this anthropological research for this ethnography on Native spirituality. I decided after my experience and insight from my spiritual journey that other people could gain from my guidance and the paths of those who participated in my research. The participants speak to a Native way of life and the insightful spiritual meaning of their personal journey.

My spiritual journey has had a deep impact on my life, as guidance from God is what brings us closer to the divine. I hope that this ethnography will bring to you as an individual a deeper understanding of the experiences of life in a different dimension from what we know and understand as physical human beings. I am not the only one who has been given insight into these matters. Those I have interviewed have also willingly shared their own experiences on their own spiritual paths. I was privileged to be able to speak with thirteen Native individuals, both men and women, from ten different Native communities. I would like to introduce them to my readers at the very beginning of my narrative, for I will be citing their words often in the pages that follow.

- Gabriel, a Yankton Sioux Elder and Medicine Man from South Dakota, has been walking his spiritual journey as a practicing medicine man for thirty-three years, and he carries the wisdom and gifts given to him by the Creator to help his people. His story is meant to be shared, and he shares it with love and goodness in his heart. He says, "I was a veteran of the Vietnam War, and I was twenty-four years old when I returned to the United States. I am now fifty-nine years old." When he returned from Vietnam in 1973, the Wounded Knee incident (see appendix) was occurring. He told me that he asked himself, "Should I go fight against the United States government at Wounded Knee, after I just came back from fighting the Vietnamese? Should I stand up and fight for my people now? And that was my struggle, because I was loyal to the United States. At the same time, I was finding my own spirit name and spirituality, and so I decided to fight for my people, with compassion—that is, to stand up and seek out our freedom, and not to live under the guides and dictation of the government."

- Marin, an Anishinaabe elder from the Mille Lacs Band of Ojibwe, is a conductor and keeper of the drum at the "Big Drum Ceremony." He shares the meaning of his responsibilities and explains the role of the Medicine Wheel[1] in this ceremony. Community sharing and feasting, drumming and singing are special amongst the Anishinaabe ceremonial people at Mille Lacs in Minnesota.

- Dawn, a Dakota woman from the Lower Sioux Reservation in Minnesota, carries the spirit name of "Recognized Woman" (Iyekiyapi win emakiyapi ye in the Dakota language). She explains through her interview how she walks her spiritual journey, showing the importance of her culture and spiritualism in her daily living. She says her spiritual journey is her whole life.

- Niko, a young man who goes by the spirit name "Lone Man," is Oglala from the Pine Ridge Reservation, South Dakota. He has been attending ceremonies such as powwows, sun dances, and sweat lodges (see Appendix) since he was fourteen years old. He reflects on the good energy, family, and ceremony that help him feel good about who he is as a Lakota and help him connect to his spiritualism.

- Talon, "Flying Eagle" (Ishpiming Migizi of the Eagle clan, Migizi dodem) is an elder affiliated with the Fond du Lac Reservation in Minnesota. On his journey, he tried many different Christian denominations until he found his way through his Native spiritual

---

1   See figure 1 at the end of this introduction for a picture of a Medicine Wheel.

journey. He speaks about his connection with a Native elder who was meant to be on his path to give him spiritual guidance and understanding in his life.

- Lara, "Rainbow Woman" of the Turtle clan, is from the Mohawks of Six Nations in Southern Ontario. She connected to her spirituality through the Iroquois traditions. The Mohawks fall under the Iroquois Six Nations, the Haudenosaunee "People of the Longhouse." She is a gifted Mohawk woman walking her spiritual journey as an ongoing quest. As she says, "Powerful all the time, could be strong in my life whether I am aware of it or not, and may not be aware of it" as she reflects on the poem called "Footprints in the Sand" written in 1936 by Mary Stevenson.

- Janika, a young woman enrolled in the Red Lake Band of Chippewa and Ho Chunk, carries the name of "White Eagle" and is of the Eagle clan. She started to understand her spiritual journey in her late teens, when she found her eagle feather out on a hike in the Duluth area.

- Teela is Cherokee and Anishinaabe and carries the spirit name of "Sky Woman" (Giizhigokwe). Teela and I passed sacred tobacco between us and her clan, the Wolf clan, came to me through spiritual guidance. She had prayed and waited a long time before her prayers were answered through spiritual guidance and the passing of sacred tobacco.

- Alexa says she is a New York Mohawk. Her spirit name, "Red-Tail Hawk Woman," was passed to her in the fall of 2006. She does not yet know her clan. She feels a connection to spiritualism that has grown since she found out about her Native ancestry. As she says, "I only recently found out about my Native lineage." She has been on her journey for about three years, and says, "The nagging has always been there, but I could not comprehend what it was, because so much of my family history was hidden." Alexa is from Minnesota.

- Leonard, Anishinaabe from Garden River First Nation in Ontario, found his spiritual path through Great White Eagle man, who passed him his spirit name "Hawk Man," or "Man who flies high in the sky with the hawks." Leonard's colors are blue, white, gray, and purple. He carries the Crane clan, and participates and conducts sweat lodge ceremonies, pipe ceremonies, and traditional talking circles (see Appendix) to help the people. He is a fire keeper dedicated to maintaining the sacred fire that connects us as a people to the spirit world and the Creator.

- Ella, an Anishinaabe woman from the Mississauga First Nation in Ontario, believes she is on a spiritual journey. As she says, "At this point in my life, gathering knowledge and wisdom from the elders and reflecting on Anishinaabe teachings helps me to understand the spirit of all."

- Forrest says he "believes life is all spirit." His spirit name is "Boss Bear," given to him by a medicine man, a spiritual guide. He is a part of the Bear clan from the Saginaw Chippewa Reservation in Michigan. He says he is also Cherokee from his grandmother's mixed Cherokee lineage. His roots go back to the frontiers of Oklahoma, where his Chippewa Cherokee grandparents traveled from Oklahoma to Saginaw. His father was Irish Catholic.

- Mabel is an Anishinaabe pipe carrier and sweat lodge conductor in her community of the Garden River First Nation in Ontario. She works to bring ceremonies, healers, and traditional teachings to her community for the Native people. Her spirit name is "Northern Lights Woman," and she carries the Bear clan as her dodem. Mabel's colors are green, brown, yellow, purple, white, and coral. Her teacher was the late Pa, a traditional man who fasted for many days to receive the vision of the Healing Lodge, which was then built. In her interview, Mabel shares her deep connection to her spiritual teacher, and describes how the traditional teachings came to her on her spiritual journey.

I have been able to touch on only a minute part of the lives of my contributors, as well as of my own spiritual journey. I realize that I will be able to bring to you only a glimpse of their lives and the spiritual journeys that each one of us walks on this earth for a short time as a human being. Life is short, but it is rich. It brings many great and fulfilling experiences that I will share with you on the next pages of this ethnography.

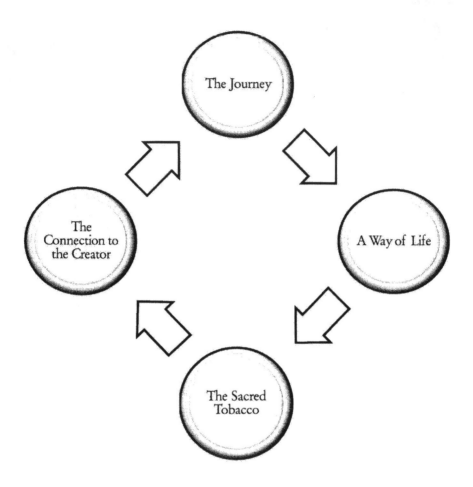

The Journey

A Way of Life

The Sacred Tobacco

The Connection to the Creator

This version of the Medicine Wheel was designed by me based on the Medicine Wheel teachings that I have attended. This particular drawing came to be a part of the explanations on Native Spirituality offered in this ethnography. (see Appendix)

Historical Influences on Native Spirituality

Historically, Native American people have been oppressed by white society. This oppression continues today as Native people struggle to revitalize their languages, cultures, and traditions and to live healthier lives. The experiences of oppression and white supremacy have been inflicted upon indigenous peoples all around the world. Hence a loss of identity and spirituality has resulted in many nations.

Before Columbus arrived in 1492, there were no peoples in the Americas known as "Indians" or "Native Americans." Each indigenous community had its own name relating to the character of its people and the lands they inhabited (Wilson, 2002, 23). Native Americans were already living in North America when the European Americans came to settle the land and subjected them to devastating experiences. By 1500, an estimated seven million to ten million Indians lived north of present-day Mexico. In the following centuries, they would face great challenges to their ways of life, values, and identities (Edmunds et al., 2007).

The European American's idea of "saving the Native" was to "kill the Indian, save the man," as the Native American people were seen as "undomesticated." Disease, famine, war, and oppression led Native American tribes to be wiped out to near extinction in North America. The Native American people who were living in civilizations across the continent were annihilated as the European Americans came to settle this land that they called the New World. Through adaptation and cultural persistence, there were tribes that survived the destruction that was visited upon the peoples who lived here. They survived through hunting and gathering and practicing traditional ways of life. The people had strong communities, and culture and tradition were the foundation of their lifestyle, which worked exceedingly well for their tribal societies. Native American people have been trying to reclaim their identities and cultures, as time has brought about some very profound changes. Many Native Americans (men, women, and children) were massacred by the United States Army. The warriors fought to protect their women, children, and elders as white settlers moved west to expand the frontier. Fraudulent treaties and broken promises led to assimilation and reservation policies that were enforced by the United States government [and the Canadian government] and led to Native American subjugation. Native Americans' spirits were broken by policies that did not allow them to retain their cultures, traditions, and languages (Edmunds et al., 2007).

Some practiced their religions underground, in darkness ceremonies, so that their spiritualism would continue on for many generations. A sense of identity and pride has slowly returned to some Native American people. Today, many have found healing, tradition, and culture to be what can balance the mind, body, and spirit. Today, the Native American people look at the four directions contained in plants, animals, the elements, and the physical, emotional, spiritual, and mental aspects of being that the Creator has provided for the people as a way of life on earth.

Many Native American people are embracing their spiritual connections and focusing on the mind, body, and spirit. Their identities as Native people are defined in the spirit and in the body, and the spiritual connection is part of the Creator and creation. Living and surviving in two worlds, the white man's world and the red man's world, they evolve within the four colors (white, red, yellow, black) of the Medicine Wheel. We are all connected in unity within the circle of life.

THE RELATIONSHIP BETWEEN
RELIGIOUS PRACTICE AND IDENTITY

According to some North American Indians, our spiritual journeys begin when our spirits unite with our bodies at conception and we develop into unique human beings. They describe this spiritual journey as walking a traditional way of life, following the ways of the past. But how do contemporary North American Indians who consider themselves traditional know and understand what it means to follow either the old or contemporary ways? This ethnography will present and analyze the ways some Native American Indians explain the very essence of Native spirituality from the past to the present, and how that defines how they walk their spiritual paths today.

Today, when Native people talk about a traditional spiritual way of life, they have in mind cultural practices that were followed prior to the arrival of non-Native settlers and Christianity. The people are also aware that these kinds of spiritual practices ceased to exist long ago. In fact, today, traditional Native spirituality has become a commodity. For example, Vine Deloria Jr. has complained about what passes for traditional Native religion today. He speaks about sweat lodges costing $50, medicine drums costing $300, and vision quests going for $500; American Indian Spirituality, he says, has grown and manifested itself in bizarre ways (Deloria 2006).

I believe Deloria is referring to the Indian people who do not remember or understand the powers that Medicine people had in the past; he is reflecting on the Indian people who continue to exploit the sacredness of ceremonies and the gifts we possess. He is letting us know that these types of exploitation exist, and the rituals do not have much meaning when they are conducted for the wrong purposes. Some Indian people today continue to practice the old ways and have the connection to the Creator, and others do not.

Today, honoraria are paid to individuals who conduct ceremonies and practice traditional healing and medicine; traditional tobacco is still prayed with and passed to the healer for the spirits. In the past, a gift such as a horse, a means of subsistence, or a form of assistance was given to the provider to demonstrate gratitude.

The assimilation of Native people into white society in our recent past has brought about the bizarre behaviors Deloria mentions. Assimilation was a time of change for Native people. Children were told they could no longer speak their language or practice their culture and traditions. They were urged to emulate white people. It was a time of physical, emotional, spiritual, and social fragmentation of all Nations.

Resistance to assimilation was different for different individuals in those dark days; some of the Native leaders rejected the Christian way of life and white education, while others accepted Christian ways, hopeful that their children would benefit and be educated. There really was no choice; assimilation was forced upon the Native people. Many Native people hid their children; many were unable to see their children for many years because boarding schools had them on twenty-four-hour a day routines involving scheduled classes in the English language, Christian religion, and domestic and trade training. The children were confined to barracks, where they had to wear uniforms. The boys had to cut their hair, which was against Anishinaabe tradition, which dictated that hair only be cut as a sign that a person had lost a loved one. These experiences at boarding schools traumatized the next generations. The impact of residential school is intergenerational. Residential school had detrimental effects on innocent children, who were exposed to many forms of abuse and neglect, with no love or nurturing. Children lost contact with their families and often could not speak to their own siblings. They lost their spiritual ways of life, languages, culture, and traditions. The documentary, *Unrepentant: Kevin Annett and Canada's Genocide,* written by Kevin Annett (producer), Lorie O'Rorke (narrator), and Louie Lawless (director) in 2006-2007 reflects on the truth behind the government and churches' cover up and the true stories told by the many survivors of residential school experience. A hard-hitting documentary that dwells on the theme of Canada's genocide. The video documents the "deliberate and systematic extermination" of non-Christian indigenous peoples within the Indian residential school system by the Catholic, United, Presbyterian and Anglican churches, in collusion with the federal government (World Cat Summary, 2011) (Annett, O'Rorke and Lawless, 2006-2007).

Today, many Native people practice both Christian and traditional ways of life. An example of the Christian influence in today's Native communities is the Native American Church (NAC), which holds meetings as frequently as every weekend. The NAC has survived as long as it has because of the strength of its community. Native American historian Bill Evans says: "The tipi [the

Native American Church] has been hard to tear down for generations. They can't tear it down, because the prayers are so strong in there" (Lassiter 1993, 240–241). There are churches in Native communities today that look very Native. For example, St. Isaac Jogues Catholic Church, a Catholic church in Sault Sainte Marie, Michigan, has a priest that is Native. By permission of the hierarchy of the Catholic Church, he provides Native traditional healings to the parishioners who attend his church. One day, some friends and I ventured across the United States and Canada International Bridge to attend a traditional healing mass at St. Isaac Jogues. When we entered, there was a line of people going up to the front of the church to receive a healing from the priest and his Native male helpers, who held sacred eagle fans in their hands. A male drummer was also singing and drumming at the front. As I walked up, I noticed many sacred items, such as eagle fans and sacred medicines of cedar and sweet grass, placed around the bottom and top of the altar. I felt the spiritual power as I moved closer to the healers and the priest. When it was my turn, they swept the wings of the eagle fans over my body as a blessing and a cleansing. The feeling was very uplifting, I felt very good and felt blessed by God. This church has both traditional and contemporary ways, the best of both worlds united as one.

Vine Deloria's criticism of the marketing of Native spirituality and my personal concerns about "assimilation" point to the many problems that exist today in Indian Country as a result of the exploitation of many Natives who claim to have spiritual powers or say they are medicine people. But at the same time, Christian and Native spirituality have become integrated, as the "Jesus Way" has found a significant place within the lives of many Native people. In *A Companion to the Anthropology of American Indians,* Thomas Biolsi reflects on the study of post-contact Native American Religions conducted by Raymond Bucko:

> Native religions were transforming themselves well before European contact. Europeans did not happen upon static religious systems, but the European incursion posed particularly difficult obstacles to the survival of Native religious traditions, while at the same time opening new avenues for religious elaboration and transformation. While government officials were more interested in cultural transformation (or "civilization") of Native peoples, Christian missionaries sought the spiritual conversion of Native Peoples to a generally European set of Christian beliefs. Religious resistance, revival, and accommodation all became important in the continuance of Native identity and survival (2004, 184).

SACRED TRADITIONAL WAYS OF
LIVING: A WAY OF LIFE

Gabriel speaks about Native spirituality today. As a practicing Yankton Sioux Medicine man from South Dakota for thirty-three years, he describes to me how things happened in the United States in previous generations:

> It was a law against our practice of our spirituality, and we could not practice it because otherwise they would send us to prison or send us to a crazy house or some place. They would not allow us to practice, so a lot of medicine people went into darkness, went into hiding and covered up all the windows and made everything dark and had their ceremonies. They were not allowed to practice their spirituality, and that was because the United States government was afraid that if the Indian people united, they would raise up and say, "Scram, Sam." They were afraid of that, but we never did, because we have always shared and we are giving people.

The law that Gabriel refers to was enacted on April 10, 1883 by the United States Federal Government and prohibited the speaking of Lakota and the practice of Lakota culture and religion (Starita 1995, 86). American Indians were not allowed to practice their spiritual way of life, until the American Indian Religious Freedom Act (AIRFA)[2] was made law on August 11, 1978. Prior to that, American Indians were imprisoned for holding Native spiritual

---

2   On and after August 11, 1978, it shall be the policy of the United States to protect and preserve for American Indians their inherent right of freedom to believe, express, and exercise the traditional religions of the American Indian, Eskimo, Aleut, and Native Hawaiians, including but not limited to access to

ceremonies. The American Indian Religious Freedom Act was passed by the United States Congress, which also issued a joint resolution that pledged to protect and preserve the traditional religious rights of American Indians, Eskimos, Aleuts, and Native Hawaiians. The AIRFA laid the groundwork for federal museums to return Native human remains and sacred objects to the American Indians and led to the passage by Congress of the Native American Graves Repatriation Act in 1990. The NAGPRA saw many sacred and culturally important objects returned to the American Indians.

For this ethnographic study on Native spirituality, I conducted semi-structured interviews and participant observations in 2007 with thirteen North American Indians who are walking their Native spiritual journeys or have in some way found a connection to their people's traditional way of life. Of course, many North American Indians continue to practice a Christian way of life, and others continue to search for their connection to the Creator. The individuals I interviewed for this ethnography speak of Native Spirituality and Christianity in many different ways.

For example, Niko, a young Lakota from Oglala, Pine Ridge reservation, South Dakota, says,

> Yeah, I think there is a connection between all religions, actually—everything from Daoism[3] to Christianity to Buddhism[4]. They are basically saying the same thing: that there is some greater being, a greater unknown. The Lakota call it the Gusala, the grandfather, but it is also the great unknown, the spirits, as nobody knows what is happening. I believe that is the same thing that happens in all religions. It is just a bunch of beliefs that people wrote down. A lot of beliefs are quite similar; if you look at Judaism[5] and Native cultures, they are almost identical. The only thing is they are separated by 1000 years and 2000 months. Christianity has a lot of the same virtues: Be one with nature, and don't take more than what you can give.

At the same time, finding a way to education through traditional forms of Native spirituality is distinct from these other traditions. Sturtevant writes about the American Indians as living in spiritual worlds very different from those of Western cultures. Differences between Christianity, Islam, and Judaism are minor compared to the religions of any North American Indian

---

sites, use and possession of sacred objects, and the freedom to worship through ceremonials and traditional rites (Laws, p. 138).

3   see Glossary for definition of Daoism.
4   see Glossary for definition of Buddhism.
5   See Glossary for definition of Judaism

societies that have distinctive cultures. American Indian religions do bear a family resemblance to each other, just as derived religions from the ancient near East are similar from a worldwide perspective (Sturtevant 1979, xi).

Within Native American societies, spiritual journeys are unique to each individual. Talon, from the Ojibwe Nation of Fond du Lac reservation in Minnesota began his spiritual journey with Christianity, but he now says that in earlier years he ran from one religion to another. Talon comments on his own life experiences with the other religions:

> I do believe I am on a spiritual journey, and I think that for a long time I fooled around and just really couldn't find myself, and I had no direction in my life whatsoever. I tried all sorts of different religions, Christian religions, and I could not find any peace or direction in any of them. As I started to learn more about Native Spirituality and some things that were shared with me by some Native people, I started to feel more comfortable with who I was in relation to my surroundings. The more I looked into it; the more I found that traditional teachings around spirituality really ring true for me in my heart, that the animals are our brothers and sisters and that we are not the most sophisticated super beings on the planet, but the most pitiful on the planet. We are dependent on everything else around us—those types of ideologies, if you would ... Yes, I think I am on a spiritual journey. There isn't a day that goes by that I don't learn more about my spirituality and who I am as a person.

Lara, a Mohawk of the Six Nations in Southern Ontario, Canada, speaks in a different way about the connection she makes between Christianity and Native Spirituality: "I feel the same spiritual presence whether I am in a long house, church, or lodge."

But Janika, Ho Chunk from her mother's side in Wisconsin and Red Lake Band of Chippewa of Minnesota from her father's side, takes the opposite position. When asked if she could see a connection between Christianity and Native Spirituality, she replied, "Not a whole lot. I guess the main thing from Christianity that turns me off is the force of ... Christian forcing religion on my Native people in the past. That it is something Native people don't do with their religion or spirituality ... Native Spirituality and Christianity don't work."

Teela, who is Cherokee and Anishinaabe from Minnesota, detects similarities between Christianity and Native Spirituality, but recalls the way Christians misunderstood Native cultural practices:

Yes, Christianity and Native Spirituality correlate easily enough for me because you know the word God and the word Creator and the word Great Mystery—to me that is all the same being. When I look at history, when the settlers first came here and called Native Americans savages, evil, devil worshippers, I think that they did not understand. They thought that they were worshipping some other God. I think that it is the same all over the world.

Leonard is Anishinaabe from the Garden River First Nation in Ontario. Putting it very simply and straightforwardly, he says that Christians and followers of Native Spirituality "are all on the same path and we are all heading in the same direction." Ella, an Anishinaabe Woman from the Mississauga First Nation in the Blind River, Ontario area, agrees with him:

> The individuals who wrote the Bible had to receive their teachings from someone, spiritual intervention; Native Spirituality received their teachings the same way, spiritual intervention, all from the spirit world. In the Bible, they had a man teacher who was able to teach moral reasoning. Native Spirituality had the similar teachings of a man who taught moral reasoning, but he used the relationship with the animals, elements, and the universe.

As my contributors have noted, some Native Americans think of Native Spirituality as a connection to all of creation. Thomas Biolsi reflects on his fieldwork on the Pine Ridge reservation from 1988 to 1990:

> At different ceremonies and at gatherings where speeches were given I frequently heard people stress that religion (or "these ways") was the last thing that the Indian people had left. While in different periods of time Native people have been identified by a variety of markers—warfare, language, kinship lines, treaties, trade, or migration—today it is clear that religion is very important to Native peoples and their identity, just as "spirituality" is one of the qualities perceived by many contemporary non-Indians to be essentially characteristic of Indians (Biolsi 2004, 171).

Anthropologist Luke Eric Lassiter explains religion as a cycle of knowledge, belief, and disbelief:

> The belief and attribution of value to supernatural beings and powers—in a word, religion—is universal among human beings; but, just like everything else that is cultural, it varies greatly. Take, for example, the Spiritist (not to be confused with "Spiritualist")

religious tradition of Brazil. The history of Spiritism or "Kardecism" is complicated, but suffice it to say that since its importation from Europe to Brazil in the late nineteenth century, it has come to combine Christian beliefs with animism (belief in spirits, which is widespread cross-culturally). Spiritism centres on the belief that dead human spirits inhabit the spirit world apart from the material world (Lassiter 2002, 167).

Sister Marianna Ableidinger, FSPA, author of the book *Integrating Ojibwe Native American and Roman Catholic Spirtualities*, explains that the purpose of her research was to show how both the Catholic and the Ojibwe traditions are enriched through dialogue and communication. She mentions that in recent years there has been growing emphasis on the recovery of Native American culture in many tribes. There has been intense dialogue between representatives of the Catholic Church and the Native Americans of the Lakota tribe, leading to recognition of the similarities of many of the rites, rituals, ceremonies, and customs of both faith traditions. The result has been a deeper shared understanding of the Lakota and the Catholic spiritualities (Ableidinger 2002).

In the Catholic Church, there are many symbols similar to those used as in the Ojibwe culture. For example, the Church has sacraments of baptism, confirmation, and the Eucharist, and blessings are given with water and the anointing with oil. Water and oil are powerful symbols of God for Catholics, and they are powerful symbols within Ojibwe cultural practices. The burning of sweet grass is used by Ojibwe people, and is used in the Church. Ojibwe use sage, cedar, sweet grass, and tobacco; these are the four sacred medicines used by Native people. Praying and sharing are found in both the Church and the Native Culture. Tobacco is put into colored cloth and tied to a Native traditional altar or other traditional sacred places, just as sacred pipes are placed on altars made of earth in sweat lodges. Tobacco is used as an offering and can stand for a promise to or a request (prayer) to the Great Spirit. The sacred tobacco is smoked in a sacred pipe. It is to bring down God's blessing on those who are praying and to send up a visible prayer (Ableidinger 2002, 8, 51).

Spirit names, clans, and personal colors are of importance to Native people who walk their spiritual journey. Their spirit names are the key to understanding their inner beings and who they are as physical beings on this earth; the names define their essence of spirit and humanness and give them a sense of who they are as Native persons. It is the Creator who gives us life on this earth, for the Creator knows each one of us as a spirit who has been given a unique life to live. We are each given a purpose and meaning in life, so in defining who we are as Native persons, we commence on a spiritual journey that the Creator has graciously bestowed upon each and every one of us.

It is with Native culture and traditions that many Native Americans have found their connections to the Creator, as the past has become part of their present within the realm of spiritualism. The journey begins from the Nations of my contributors, who participate willingly as they share their spirit names, their clans, and their colors. Their names and clans have been spiritually passed to them from the Creator through a spiritual medicine person or pipe carrier, or their clans have been passed from their mother's or father's lineage, depending on their tribal traditions and teachings. For some, their clans cannot be linked to their lineage, as there is a break that severed their ties to their family clan system as a consequence of European American forced assimilation. When this is the case, their clans must be sought through spiritual prayer with the Creator.

Through the Creator, we can be fulfilled with love and life, as this comes from above; we ask for our lives from the Creator. We put our life to use, as it is ours and he has put us in control of it. The Earthmaker gave us the means of obtaining a good life; we control our lives and so does every single spirit that he created. Therefore we must concentrate our minds on the Creator. Be assured that he will not take anything from us without giving something in return; we then pour out handfuls of tobacco for him, as he will take it and not reject it (Beck 1992, 40).

Dawn, a Dakota woman from the Lower Sioux Reservation, discusses the sacred way of life she has been given by the Creator. She was named "Recognized Woman" (Iyekiyapi win emakiyapi ye in the Dakota language), and she defines her life as follows:

> My spiritual journey is my whole life. At least the way I was taught, I was born into the family that I was born into and the family that I have was decided by the Creator. The person who named me, I didn't know well; the name is just the continuant. He prays and the Creator tells him what the name is, and he tells me what the Creator said. It's amazing, for this gentleman not knowing us all that well, how right on the names were; they fit our personalities. He named my sister, my aunt, and a number of people in my family; he didn't know us very well. Knowing what my name is has helped me to navigate; knowing what my name is will help me make decisions and navigate.

Another sacred connection that occurred was with Mabel, an Anishinaabe woman from the Garden River First Nation in Ontario. She shares how her spirit name, clan, and colors came to her through her spiritual experience with her spiritual elder:

> It was nighttime and the northern lights, white beams of light, visual dancing, colored lights, appeared, and I could visualize the sacred fire; the lights reminded me of it. We both went to the Elders' Gathering on education; who we are was talked about, and how it is important. Get your name, colors, and clan, and you will know when the time is right. Elders focused on the same topics and the same importance. You will know when you know. From that point on, no base of time, it started one day and knowing, I went to Pa and passed tobacco and gave him tobacco; what he did was right then and there. We went to Echo Bay with feast food, and got wine (Maria Christina). On the trip up there, he said, "Your name could be this and that."
>
> "What does that mean?"
>
> He said, "Whatever, okay, yeah."
>
> We were driving farther; then it came as "Northern Lights Woman." I felt a tingle through my whole body and a flash back to him. When we came back from the Elders' Gathering, there was a teaching about alcohol; a strong spirit takes over your spirit, it takes you and there is a ceremony to take your spirit back. After that, a dream came about my clan. In the dream I was a tall man with buckskin in an old cabin, in there with a bear. The bear asked for me to shoot it, and I said, "I can't shoot you," and instead cut the bear's claws. Then I had recurring dreams of bears between me and my kids. The Bear is my dodem[6]; my clan came to be Bear." In a dream vision, the history of my clan system went too far back in my family—mom, grandfather, and their lineage. No way to go back to find it, who my clan was. My colors came to pass through a couple who were visionaries. I have two to three more colors since; they progress when you are ready. My colors are green, brown, yellow, purple, white, and coral.

Maria Christina wine had symbolic meaning during a gathering when Mabel had a spiritual experience. She did not know the Ojibwe language that the spiritual elder was speaking in, nor was she a public speaker. But

---

6   Dodem means clan in the Ojibwe language.

through her spiritual experience, she understood the language, cried, and stood up and spoke the words, "Holy Mary, Mother of God, pray for us sinners now and at the hour of our death," and connected to the elder's teachings just moments before he ended his words of wisdom. As this spiritual encounter brought Mabel to speak out and relate to the elder's teachings, as she understood the Ojibwe words that he spoke, the spirit moved her to speak out the "Hail, Mary." Some of the Native people at the Elder's gathering would have understood the Ojibwe language, and would have related to the connection, and others may have heard and related only to Mabel's words spoken in the English language. A connection of words spoken in both Ojibwe and English defined the meaning of the teaching that was passed on at the Elders' Gathering, where many Ojibwe people had gathered.

Reflecting on the life of Gabriel, who became a practicing medicine man, provides us with the answer to the question, "Have the old ways really been swept away by the wind?" Gabriel speaks about his spiritual guidance in the following way:

> Through Martin's ceremonies, they presented a pipe to me when I was a young man; that pipe is what got me started. I knew it was sacred, but I did not know what it meant. I didn't want to make any mistakes or make a mockery of it, so I took my time before I took it out. I must have had it for three or four years before I started to use it, and I went around to the elders asking questions about the pipe: What is it, this pipe? What do I do? What am I supposed to do? Finally, that is when I started meeting all of these older medicine men, like George, Robert, Charlie, Martin, and Crowdog. The old man Leonard, not only Leonard but his father, I met and visited and talked to, and Albert was one of my connections. These men, these spiritual men, started telling me things about the Native ways and culture, and each gave me something I needed. So my journey's been guided all along. I have to look back and reflect and see. Since then, I have been through ceremonial ways; I was yuwipi,[7] where they tied you up, to do the ceremony, and the spirits told me to do that. So I did that, and the yuwipi man, that was difficult, that was hard to do. But now today, I still go to the mountains and fast.
>
> And the bundle [Gabriel received an elk dream; the elk is a symbol of love that carries six or seven medicines and is carried for emotional healing and financial help. It helps you grow, get stronger and healthier] has a lot of information and knowledge that comes from other sources around the world, and my journey

---

7   See appendix.

has led me around the world. So I've been to Egypt, I have been to Hawaii, and I've prayed with the Kahoka over there, and in Egypt and Cairo. I prayed at the pyramid there and in South America. I prayed with the medicine people in South America at a spiritual gathering where my son was born, and his birth was the symbol of the fulfillment of the prophecy, which is: When the eagle from the North comes together with the condor of the South, there will be peace between the continents. So that little boy was recognized as a grandfather who came back to help the people; Jeremiah is with us today, and he comes from the Yankton Sioux nation.

In my fastings, the spirits come to talk to me; there was a deer spirit that came into one and walked up to the altar when I was sitting on the altar, and it said to me, I am the Chief of all these black tales here. In that bundle, you have high children, and if they don't come to ceremonies—and he put his head down, and in his horns he picked up the bundle and then offered it to the four directions, and to God and to Mother Earth, and then put it down. And then he turned around, and then he left. After that, I was not afraid to say that I was a medicine man; that was actually one of my visions that I have had many, many of those experiences like that, when the spirits come and talk to you and take you to places. My connection with the God is very extensive.

The yuwipi ceremony shared by Gabriel, medicine man from South Dakota, is a prime example of the strong and powerful ceremonies that are practiced by medicine people of today. It tells us that we have not lost our old ways; our old ways are within us. We just need to find what the Creator has put in front of us, and go with that belief and understand that our Native spirituality is a very strong and powerful connection to the Creator. Listening to the stories told by my study participants reveals to us a spiritual path that is guided by a higher power, the Creator.

To walk a good way of life is to walk it with respect for all people and all of creation, so those who dishonor Native Spirituality without proper motives must have hard lessons to learn in life. The ones who practice Indian ways in the form of bizarre behaviors, as described by Vine Deloria Jr. (2006), only define themselves as a group of people who have not found the connection and who walk in a way that indicates that their rituals are not rituals and are not genuine. Nor could those behaviors be recognizable to spirits, as they already know the means and motives of such behaviors well before the practitioners know their own motives for imitating traditional rituals and ceremonies.

The sacredness[8] of ceremonies and how that is perceived by the Creator and the spirits is told to us by the sacred medicine people, chosen people who carry the powers and gifts to hear the Creator and the spirits who speak to them. It is the people who fabricate traditional rituals that continue to put the riches of the material world ahead of the Creator; these people have hard lessons to learn, as the Creator puts before us lessons in life that we are meant to learn in our human lives, and it is our inner being that connect us spiritually to the Creator. If we do not learn the lessons, they will reoccur in our lifetimes, until we have learned what we were meant to learn, as spirits having a human experience. Our choices in life can manifest tenfold when we make good choices to help others in kind ways, but when bad choices are made toward others, a tenfold manifestation occurs.

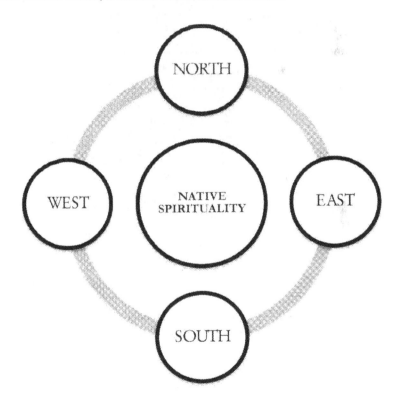

This connection to the Creator and creation is found for example within the teachings of the Medicine Wheel[9] as explained by Gabriel, the Yankton Dakota Medicine Man:

---

8   See Glossary for sacred and sacredness.
9   See Glossary for Medicine Wheel.

I will tell you about living a balanced lifestyle; you live a balance lifestyle by taking a look at your family: How is it that you get along in your family? How do you take care of your family? How are your children, and how have things been? Then figure out how everybody is happy and they feel good, and all that. Then on to the next, and you look at your finances. Today you have finances, ways to manage your monies, how to make the most out of what you have; it's natural prosperity, it's divine prosperity for you that you have been given, and it is your responsibility to take that prosperity and to use it the best. And when you've researched it and studied it and looked after it, what you need is for you to find a balance, and then you move on to the next. Where you go from there is to your spirituality. So in today's times, spirituality, you look at how often you practice your spirituality. Well, in my life, we both go to a sun dance once a year, we both fast once a year, we both go to sweat lodges as often as we can, and we have ceremonies as often as we can; it tends to help us to keep a balance in life. And then your culture is cultural things, singing and dancing, and is part of your next step, which is your spirituality understood. You know where it's at and you feel good with it, then you go on to the next one. And then you go to the fourth color in the Medicine Wheel—black, white, yellow, and red—then you're taking care of yourself when you take care of yourself, your emotions, your physicalness, your health, your well-being; you understand your body, there are many many things for you to grow within this journey of taking care of yourself.

Some Native people today understand and know their Native Spirituality, while some people are just learning or continue to learn. When there is no spiritual acceptance by some Native people within the "circle" of spiritual seekers, then the people who do not accept have lessons to learn, if they do not acknowledge the ways of the Creator. The Creator knows and will help them find their way, if they choose to do so. They just need to ask for guidance from the Creator to find their way along their spiritual paths. The Medicine Wheel holds the teachings passed to us from our ancestors and the Creator. We should respect and accept all people in the world, as the four directions of the Medicine Wheel honor the white in the north direction, yellow to the east, red to the south, and black to the west, representing the four colors of all humans in the world. The Native people are referred to as the red people on the Medicine Wheel. If the medicine people and healers are following the Medicine Wheel teachings to help others heal and for their own spiritual path, they know and understand these meanings. It is in this way of life that we practice the teachings of the four directions of the Medicine Wheel, in keeping with the beliefs of our ancestors, and the teachings the Creator has provided to the Native people.

My interview subjects for this ethnography know what Native spirituality is, as the Medicine people and healers know their purpose in life. It is through these Medicine people, who understand the spiritual journey of our Native people that guidance is given to those who follow the traditional Native ways of living.

Ella, an Anishinaabe medicine woman from Mississauga First Nation says, "My spirit journey began when I was a little girl, listening to elders, grandparents talk about who we are ... not fully understanding but knowing, just knowing that there was some kind of connection to what I did not understand during that time. This created a connection to the forest, to the animals, to creation."

"Everything is laid out for you. Your path is straight ahead of you. Sometimes it's invisible but it's there. You may not know it's going, but still you have to follow that path. It's the path to the Creator that's the only path there is" (Arden 1990, 106).

Ceremonies are attended by Native people of many nations, and in Minnesota these include the Big Drum ceremonies that are held throughout the territory of the Mille Lacs Band of Ojibwe. The Big Drum ceremony is "simple but means a lot," according to Marin, an elder and conductor of the Big Drum ceremony, which I attended on June 16, 2007. In lower Minnesota, there is the Pipestone sun dance ceremony, which in 2007 completed its seventeenth Annual Gathering of the Sacred Pipes. It was held from July 27, 2007 to August 5, 2007, and attracted over two hundred Native people. These were mostly Dakota and Lakota people, but other nations, such as the Ojibwe people from Canada, attended as well. Many other ceremonies are practiced by the Anishinaabe people and other nations today. Leonard, an Ojibwe fire keeper from Garden River, Ontario, has attended pipe ceremonies, sweat lodge ceremonies, sunrise ceremonies, sacred fire ceremonies, rain dances and ghost dances, windego (clown) ceremonies, black room ceremonies, shaky tent ceremonies, birthing ceremonies, drumming ceremonies, funeral ceremonies, and ghost feasts.[10] Leonard has attended the ceremonies mentioned on his spiritual path; I have participated in some of the ceremonies he conducted, and I see a man who carries the spirit of the hawk, a messenger, and who is of the Crane Clan, which symbolizes leadership. He dedicates his time and energy to the people. He knows how sacred the fire is, and he spends his days and nights tending the sacred fire he started with his flint for the very purpose of helping others. Sacred fires are burned during ceremonies, for

10   The ceremonies mentioned are listed in the glossary.

people out on fasts, or for the death of a loved one and the grieving families. The sacred fire allows us to have a deeper connection to the Creator and the spirit world. Ceremonies are performed with sacredness by the people who know the protocol and ways of the ceremonies, and who are guided by spirit. Leonard says, "Ceremony helps me to connect to nature, and my own inner being." A young man by the name of Niko describes attending ceremony as "something you just can't read in a book; it's once you're there, there is a huge energy in it, you take energy from the family around you and the ceremony around you."

There are ceremonies that are held specifically for women, such as the Grandmother Moon ceremony that Dawn, a Dakota woman, speaks about as "a way for women to get together and support one another," adding that "the moon is important to us" and that "women don't need to sweat because of the way the Creator made us." Then there are some people such as Lara, a Mohawk from Six Nations in Southern Ontario, who does not wish to talk about her spiritual path: "Sacredness—should not talk about it, it wouldn't feel right."

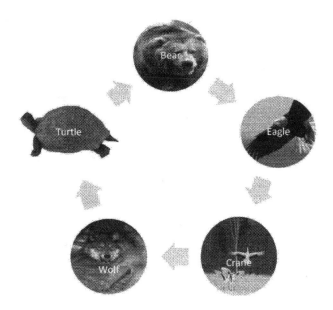

The Clans of My Informants, I have only mentioned five clans, there are many more such as the weasel, hawk, fish, lynx, whale, otter, beaver, moose, deer, buffalo, and so forth.   As all is cyclical in nature as in the medicine wheel, so are the clans that are mentioned giving a circular motion between the clans as the arrows shown are connecting the cycle of nature.

Thirteen Informants rated themselves on a scale of 0-7 where 7 is the highest rating, 0 being the lowest. This rating was completed from their own personal views of where they saw themselves on their spiritual journeys, without making comparisons to each.

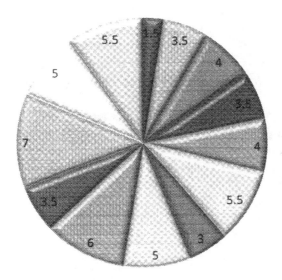

There are contentious areas of study for anthropologists studying Native religions. Anthropologist Thomas Biolsi writes:

> There is a contention in the Native community over who in fact may speak authoritatively about Native religion—both in terms of access to accurate knowledge, and in terms of the ethics of those made powerful by colonial history (anthropologists) presuming to speak for those marginalized by colonial history. Related to this is the question of what kinds of knowledge are appropriate for recording. Barbara Owl, a White Earth Anishinaabe, states: We have many particular things which we hold internal to our cultures. These things are spiritual in nature, and they are for us, not for anyone who happens to walk in off the street. They are ours and they are not for sale. Because of this, I suppose it's accurate to say that such matters are our "secrets," the things which bind us together in our identities as distinct peoples. It's not that we never make outsiders aware of our secrets, but we—not they—decide what, how much, and to what purpose this knowledge is to be

put … Everything else has been stripped from us already (Biolsi 2004: 173).

This is a personal preference and choice made by some American Indians not to speak about their spiritualism; it is not the only choice. As Barbara Owl from White Earth says there are "secrets" and are not to be shared, Gabriel, Yankton Sioux Medicine Man for thirty-three years, speaks about his spiritual path with such dignity and passion that he inspires his followers, who find that he lifts their spirits to higher enlightenment. When he speaks about ceremonies, he says, "Sweat lodges and fasting and preparing for the sun dance ceremony is one year in advance and that the dancers pledge the four days of fasting and dancing and praying for the people, so that we can live." Gabriel said, "How the spirits work the ceremonies, when they took it out of the darkness and into the light. We needed to come into the light because the darkness is what held us back all these years."

My subjects were asked why they thought some Native people were open to sharing ceremonies and teachings, and others were not open to sharing Native spirituality. A few people shared Leonard's point of view: "People that share usually have lots to share with what they learn, and people that don't really don't have anything, and don't like sharing. For those that are not open, it is because some people get stuck in the residential school stuff[11], and some just don't care." He tells us that Tibetan monks, priests, professors, doctors, coaches, a psychiatrist, judges, and people of disparate cultures (including Asian American and African American and countries (China, Japan, Spain, and Brazil, for example) have participated at the Garden River sweat lodges.

Ella, a Mississauga medicine woman, responded to my question with:

Being open to the teachings, that depends on where you have received your teachings from … sometimes elders who are very open to the historical content of when the Europeans first came here and what they had lost … this would imply that it is okay to share with others … they lost connection to the land … and so to share what

---

11 "Residential school stuff" is referring to enforced assimilation, the goal of which was to change the Indian into a white person. People were subjected to a loss of identity in language, culture, and traditions at boarding schools up to the mid-1900s. Children were taken from their parents and homelands to faraway schools, where they were enrolled in a twenty-four-hour schooling system, and later day schools on the reservations. Today, they still reflect on the abuse and assimilation, which has had an intergenerational effect on the nations.

they lost ... is part of their spirituality. They still have maintained their spiritual beliefs ... but the connection to the land is very limited ... Individuals who are open to this concept of sharing Native Spirituality are the ones who understand history ... in this manner they come to an understanding based on the teachings and prophecies ... that a time would come when people from other areas would travel to our land and how we treated them would be based on the concept of the seven grandfather teachings.

Forrest says:

I think that each person is where they are suppose to be, and I am going to do as I do, and walk in the spirit and then if they see that, and they see what that brother has, then they want that, each person comes into their own spirituality in their own time. Each person is given their gift; I have the gift of gab, I have the gift of influence. There are things I don't talk about, and I want to very much, but practicing that is all part of walking the red road.

Mabel, pipe carrier from Garden River First Nation has a different view of things:

Personally, what has happened stemming from the era of residential schools impacts non-Native prophesy. If they come with brotherhood and friendship, and with gifts, as many of the Spanish came with rifles in search of brotherhood, conditioning from this is being protective of it. They came to steal gold and riches, no teaching about it. Things that all the leaders at this point were told was to not show them anything shiny, to always remember who we are; [it] all made sense as to being careful of what we give as information.

FEASTS

Whether we share our spiritualism or choose to stay private with it, we who are on our spiritual journeys will continue to practice our Native Spirituality. Part of this includes sharing and feasting, which are very important functions of ceremonies. Not only do participants feast our spirits in the physical world, we also feast the spirits in the spirit world. Feasts involve the consumption of traditional foods prepared by mostly women. As it has always been, food preparation is the responsibility of the women of the tribe. During the Big Drum ceremony with the Mille Lacs Band of Ojibwe, for example, feast food called "spirit dishes" is prepared by the warrior women; this was explained to me by Marin, an Elder who conducted the ceremony. In this ceremony, women are also the keepers of the drum and members of the band; these women are recognized as keepers, and are honored with specific traditional songs from the drummers. They stand during that time, and dance in position. Near the end of the ceremony, wild rice that was prepared by the warrior women is served to all the people in the lodge, feasting their spirits.

Marin explained the importance of sharing not just food but also tobacco, which serves as a means of communication between the physical world and the spiritual world. Sharing and gift giving is a special way of life for most American Indian people, as it is with gifts that one is blessed by the Creator. The sacred tobacco is prayed with to communicate to the Creator and spiritual beings from the spirit world, penetrating the veil, as it is known, between our world and the spirit world. Communicating with tobacco is the way our prayers are heard; it is a link to the other side. The gifts are always a part of the ceremonies and interaction between Native people; they represent an act of reciprocity. Giving gifts is also a way to honor human beings. In June of 2007, I honored the Elder Marin during my ethnographic research. I passed him a woven blanket embellished with animals, as I was grateful for the time and energy he had put into assisting me throughout the day, while I documented and participated in the sacred big drum ceremony. The look on his face and in his eyes when he received the blanket was enough for me to know that he appreciated his gift.

Sacred Tobacco—Prayer

One of the technical elements of rituals, and ceremonials in general, is prayer. Prayers can be spoken, chanted, whispered, or sung; they can be accompanied by ritual actions, done in special places with altars, or spoken alone in the woods without anything but silence. Prayers can be made by individuals alone or by groups of people together. The words are carefully chosen and carefully listened to, so that the force of the words and the images behind them travel between the speaker and the other individuals to become one thought. We might call this group consciousness "collective mindfulness," because in these instances, each individual's thoughts are directed to a collective thought and collective objectives (Beck 1992, 39).

When I met the Elder Marin at the Ceremonial building at the Mille Lacs reservation, I passed tobacco to him for spiritual information about the Big Drum ceremony. I prayed with the tobacco before I passed it to him; then he acknowledged the tobacco and placed it into the basket by the big drum. Native people pray by passing tobacco between themselves and a spiritual person, such as a medicine person, who can assist them with their spiritual journey. It is offered while praying to the Creator and the spirits. Native people give up prayers by putting sacred tobacco into the sacred fire,[12] into the water, and onto the earth, and with the sacredness of prayer, the person praying is in touch with the Creator. My study subjects speak about the role of tobacco in sharing about their spiritualism. Tobacco was shared between Talon and his spiritual helper Dorothy, as she shared spiritual guidance for Talon on his

---

12   Sacred fire is the element in the physical world that connects us to the Creator and the spirit world. It is started by a fire keeper, who is a man. The fire keeper carries a flint that he uses to start the fire. Most Native spiritual people pray to the fire, feast at the fire, hold ceremonies around the fire, and make a connection through the element of fire. The fire is a direct spiritual connection.

journey. Dorothy said, "I am going to share some things with you, but first you have to offer me some tobacco." Doing her own house blessing, Teela prayed and set out her tobacco onto Mother Earth, by a tree.

Alexa reflects on her ritual of prayer:

> I don't pray the way I was taught to pray as a child. When I pray I don't ask for monetary things; I mostly pray for guidance. I am more aware when I ask for strength that comes to me through spirituality. It is hard to unlearn what you are taught as a child, going to the church and getting on your knees at the end of the bed. I was taught that prayer was a private thing and it's not, and there is strength in prayer if it is done properly. You know not to ask for monetary things; I don't ask for things for me anymore; I ask for things for other people. I think it makes me more aware.

Leonard reflects on the people who attend the sweat lodges he conducts: "We encourage people to pray in their own language, no matter who they are." Leonard puts tobacco in the lodge if they call for it, and people give tobacco for whatever they are asking for at the sweat lodge. During the sun dance ceremony, there is an act of sacrifice, and there is prayer for the people through dance, drum, and song. There are medicines, pipes, sacred items, dreams, vision quests, and the spirits that intertwine in spiritual connections. Mabel talks about her gifts coming through the power of prayer. She communicates with the stone nation[13]. She can hear, see, feel, and speak things, and she keeps within her heart what the Creator has put in her heart. She reflects on smudging with sweet grass, tobacco, cedar, and sage, the four sacred medicines used in a ritual to purify oneself. She says, "To walk the Red Road[14] is to follow the guidance each day, to get up and put tobacco out. There are certain things to do spiritually that are important to follow, that keep balance on the earth. [We should] do offerings and be grateful for what the Creator did for us."

As a Native person walking my own spiritual journey, I had been praying for help, so I passed tobacco to Gabriel, the medicine man, for spiritual healing. I was aware of negative energies that had been surrounding me, preventing my spiritual growth. My spiritual growth is important as my spiritualism enables me to help people. I visited him at his home following the sun dance ceremony, and there he did his healing work on me with his

---

13   The stone nation consists of the rocks or stones that are found on Mother Earth that carry her spirit. They speak to Mabel, as she has the gift to communicate with the stone nation.

14   The Red Road is the road that most Native people walk, and it leads them to the Creator. This is referred to as a Native Spiritual journey.

wife as his helper using his sacred bundles. With frankincense oil [that God provided to Jesus at birth through the wise men], and using the medicine of the clown, I was healed of the daunting entities that had been literally making me ill; I was healed at the time of this negativism during this healing ritual. Praying and healing work hand in hand, and God works through powerful ways and powerful people answering your prayers.

As a Native anthropologist seeking spiritual experiences and knowledge, I passed tobacco ties to those of whom I made requests. A tobacco tie is a piece of red broad cloth cut into squares of three to four inches and filled with tobacco and prayed with; then the cloth square is tied with yarn, to form a small sack. I prayed and passed a tobacco tie to each person I interviewed. This ritual helped me and each person I interviewed to experience a spiritual sharing between us. As the interview subjects heard the spiritual message that was passed to them through me, they connected to their own understanding of it; they understood why they had received the words that I shared with them. For example, one person I interviewed, Talon, understood why I passed him tobacco. As he said, "You gave me tobacco today because we are going to talk about some spiritual things; that's the way our people do things." He explained that on his spiritual journey, he had met the Native woman named of Dorothy from Fond du Lac, who has since passed on; he describes his encounter with her as follows:

> She said, "I am going to share some things with you about who you are, but first you have to offer me some tobacco. You don't ask why, you just do it." She started sharing some things about who I was as a person, not that she could read my mind. She talked about what our ancestors had in common; the more she talked about the culture, the language, and the spirituality, you could not deal with one without the other two.

Teela, a Cherokee and Anishinaabe woman whose spirit name is Sky Woman (*Giizhigokwe* in Ojibwe), says the spirit world "is what some people call a veil between this world and the other side, and sometimes we are not given any glimpses of the other side, and sometimes and especially some people who are very sensitive have a lot of communication with the other side."

Communicating through prayer is how we communicate across the veil to ask for help in our physical world; it gives us guidance into our lives, and a better understanding of our spiritual journeys.

SACRED ITEMS

In the book *Wisdomkeepers*, Mathew King, Lakota, speaks about the power of the pipe:

> I've got Red Cloud's peace pipe. They gave me that when they made me a Chief. I wouldn't accept it in the beginning. He's a great man. He made all those treaties. He fought when he had to and beat the White Man's soldiers, wiped Custer out. He had a lot of powers. But I'd rather solve my problems through peace. I also have Black Bear's pipe and Noble Red Man's. The Peace Pipe is our only weapon. It's our holy power. It's God's power. The Pipe mediates between man and God. To receive the Pipe, to receive God's gift, you've got to be pure in your heart, mind, body, and soul. And never forget that after the prayers you've got to live that life, a life with God that's the hardest part (Beck 1992, 30–31).

The traditional ways and spiritual journeys are there for the many Native people who wish to walk their Native paths to the Creator, who has provided the ways and tools for us to help one another and help the earth, water, and environment for the next seven generations. The tools include medicines, sacred pipes, tobacco, feathers, and any sacred artifacts that might be viewed as sacred items and are carried in a bundle. Most Native people see the world through the symbolic meanings of the Medicine Wheel and Medicine Wheel teachings, as these are ways of keeping the aspects of our spiritual, emotional, physical, and mental well-being in balance.

THE CREATOR, THE JOURNEY

How do we explain our lives on earth as physical human beings, as we have been put here to fulfill a life given to us by God, to whom we refer as the Creator of all creation? It is through prayer that we connect to God, and it is with listening that we know the path that has been chosen for us. As spirits, we have come to live as human beings to learn the lessons that have been put before us. Through ceremony, we make our connection to the spirits and spirit world and our connection to God. In the Big Drum Ceremony that he conducted, the Elder Marin says, "the men who were speaking in Ojibwe were praying and giving thanks to the Creator and spirit, thanking him for sacred things." We need to reflect and take time to think about God. Janika says she needs to take time to breathe; when she is really busy, she doesn't feel connected. Teela says that the Native Spiritual path "was so perfect for me and so simple and fulfilling is the gift of Creator, and it does help a person live a good life."

In the sun dance ceremony, I saw a male dancer kneel beside the sacred tree; the symbol of the Creator in the centre of the ceremonial grounds; he was in deep prayer. Gabriel, the medicine man from South Dakota, speaks about God in the context of the commandments that he made for us to follow: "Thou shalt not kill, thou shalt not steal, thou shalt not covet thy neighbors. God made all of these commandments, and he speaks about world peace coming to this planet, and that world peace is going to come; it's on its way." How does Gabriel know and understand that world peace is on its way? He has a connection to God. God tells him, and he listens to God. Knowing the ways of our Native people is to know and understand that God is guiding our paths; all we have to do is listen.

Geronimo was a holy man in his time (1823 to 1909). He was a Chiricahua Apache, a great warrior whose greatness was enhanced by his special abilities as a war shaman (Hollihan 2002, 130). It took three-quarters of the standing American army to capture him. One of Geronimo's warriors speaks about the immense medicine powers he witnessed:

> When he was on the warpath, Geronimo fixed it so that morning wouldn't come too soon. He did it by singing. Once we were going to a certain place, and Geronimo didn't want it to become light before he reached it. He saw the enemy while they were in a level place, and he didn't want them to spy on us. He wanted morning to break after we had climbed over a mountain, so that the enemy couldn't see us. So Geronimo sang, and the night remained for two or three hours longer. I saw this myself (Deloria 2006, 206–207).

I speak about Geronimo because he was a great Chief in his time and carried the powers of a medicine man, and with this we can see the connection that some Native people of today have with these gifts to heal and see into the future; they may possess gifts that take their spirits on a spiritual journey. The past meets the present-day Native spiritualism of our people through dreams, visions, spiritual experiences, and connections to the spirit world and the Creator.

In more recent times, I met Betty J. Eadie just outside Chapleau, Ontario at a Native Women's Gathering, where she told us of her near-death experience following her hysterectomy:

> I reached for the cord near the bed in an attempt to call the nurse. But try as I might, I could not bring myself to move. I felt a terrible sinking sensation, like the very last drops of blood were drained from me. I heard a soft buzzing sound in my head and continued to sink until I felt my body become still and lifeless. Then I felt a surge of energy. It was almost as if I felt a pop or release inside me, and my spirit was suddenly drawn out through my chest and pulled upward, as if by a giant magnet. My first impression was that I was free. There was nothing unnatural about the experience. I was above the bed, hovering near the ceiling. My sense of freedom was limitless, and it seemed as if I had done this forever. I turned and saw a body lying on the bed (Eadie 1992, 37–39).

Eadie talks about the three men that appeared to her spirit, ancient men that carried great spirituality, knowledge, and wisdom. She says, "They had been with me for eternities," and through them, she saw that death was actually a "rebirth into a greater life of understanding and knowledge that stretched forward and backward through time" (Eadie 1992, 40).

This dying experience is God's way of connecting us, and it has given me insights into my own life. I have spoken previously about a dying experience in my twenties, during which I passed over to the spirit world. I was in a boat out fishing on the water, and on the return to shore at dark; I sitting at the back of the boat, full of laughter and laughing at a song that a male occupant of the boat was singing. I recall that I had a sharp pain in the right side of my head, and grabbed my head in pain. Then I was above the boat suspended over the top of what seemed to be a white fog, but there was no fog; it was dark. I could see myself lying over the back end of the boat and voices saying, "Take her to shore; take her to shore." After hearing the yelling, I was whisked away very quickly to another dimension. I heard drumming. I passed into the spirit world; I went through the tunnel of darkness, and seemed to be in flight, flying around groups of people in circles, everywhere, many, many circles of people who were faceless. Some groups were large, and some were very small. Then I noticed a face of a man I knew from the physical world who had died from a cancerous brain tumor; his name was Lucas. I knew I was in a space at the edge of an astonishing light. Many things were passing through my thoughts. I knew I was not suppose to be there, it was not my time. A wordless panic seemed to overcome me, as I was now aware of where I had journeyed. I lowered my head where I sat, and as I wondered what it meant, a voice very softly spoke my name, "Judy." At that moment, I lifted my head to look at who had called my name. I had returned to my body, to the boat where I left my body lying, but now I had a person yelling in my face and shaking me: "Judy, Judy!" I said, "What?" very quietly, as if to answer the voice I had heard call my name so softly, and then I told the people in the boat that I had just gone someplace.

This was God's way of waking me up, as I have a journey to fulfill that is much greater than I can ever imagine. It was my awakening and the beginning of a spiritual journey that will last a lifetime, well into my elderly years. Spiritual insights have been passed to me, and I have experienced insights to walk on earth as a medicine woman. I have been spiritually acknowledged as a Clan Mother through the shaky tent ceremony, and a Grandmother to many in my elderly years. The shaky tent conductor told me that I was chosen by God a long time ago. What does this mean? Does this mean that through God's guidance, I will be able to bring hope and inspiration to people?

Native Spirituality is what keeps a people strong, connected to the Creator and creation, and walking a good way of life. It was this way that the late Elder Edith, from a remote Oji-Cree community in Northern Ontario, gave me as an understanding of the powerful gifts that God grants to us as humans to help others. Edith had the gift to see your past, present, and future. God had sent me to her to learn about Edith's life and Native ways. Edith carried the gift to journey to the spirit world while she was a human being alive on Earth; her spirit could pass beyond to the spirit world without being turned back as some who journey are turned away because it is not their time. Edith journeyed to the spirit world to gain knowledge required in the physical world. She had a gift to spirit travel, which is my gift as well; I journey to the dimension outside our physical world, which is the spirit world, or what some call heaven. Native spirituality is a journey that many Native people know about today, but it is also for the Native people who lost their way and who can still find their spiritual paths and connection to God and the people God puts on their paths. Native spirituality is a journey that leads you toward a more fulfilled human experience as a spiritual being.

Appendix—Sacred Ceremonies/Images

The following explanations are provided to give you a better understanding of what types of ceremonies are being held today. There are descriptions of sacred ceremonies held by Native people in different geographical areas, including those held by the Mille Lacs Band of Ojibwe in Minnesota, the sacred ceremonies held with the Anishinaabe in the Sault Ste. Marie area in Ontario, and the Dakota ceremonies in lower Minnesota and South Dakota. A ceremony is held with respect and sacredness. People participate and a conductor leads the ceremony, praying with tobacco to the sacred fire and through smoking tobacco in the sacred pipes. The conductor may have helpers throughout the ceremony. An event can be a normal get-together to do other things outside of ceremonial gatherings.

- **Big Drum Ceremony**—This is an Ojibwe drum ceremony. Five or more male drummers sit around a big drum and sing Ojibwe ceremonial songs, passed to them by the Great Spirit or from others. The drum is a Sioux drum that was passed to the Mille Lacs Band drummers by the Sioux nation, according to Marin, the Elder at the Mille Lacs Band of Ojibwe. Blankets are hand made by the women who attend the ceremony and are divided into piles. They are prayed on by the drummers and community members in attendance, and may be used to gather tobacco and any money that may be donated to the people from the other two reserves of the Mille Lacs Band who have come to the ceremony. Feast food is prepared by the women and is shared with the community people in attendance. Songs are sung for the keepers of the drums, some of whom are women. Each woman stands up and dances where she is standing when her song is sung. This is the women's position as sacred keepers of the drum. The Big Drum Ceremony commences on a Friday, when the first feast goes on from 5:00 p.m. to 8:00 p.m., and is continued again on Saturday from 10:00 a.m. until 12:00 midnight. Drummers come from all over, and gifts are shared with the drum keepers (Mille Lacs Big Drum Ceremony, June 16, 2007).

- **Drumming Ceremony**—Women participate in singing and drumming at the Healing Lodge in Garden River, Ontario. Sacred songs are sung in the Ojibwe language while sacred pipes are smoked. A sacred fire burns in the centre of the lodge in a fire pit that is circular. It is a time of prayer through song, smoking the sacred pipes, and praying with tobacco to the sacred fire. Spirits are feasted, and feast food is shared by all in attendance. It is women who drum on hand drums; anywhere from one to several women will participate in the drumming. It is different from the Big Drum Ceremony at Mille Lacs, as it is the men who sit at the big drum. The men's drum is also used in the ceremony at the healing lodge, but I have specifically noted the women here because women drum and sing more frequently at the Garden River First Nation healing lodge. The teaching of the drum comes from the women, and today it is the women who will bring the change. My personal spiritual mission, provided in the guidance I received from the shaky tent is to make a traditional drum that is the diameter of my arm and as deep as the length from my fingertips to my elbow, a big drum for ceremonial purposes (Personal Experiences, 1990–2011).

- **Birthing Ceremony**—This ceremony offers the participant an experience of feeling the journey of being birthed. A person will sometimes struggle through the birth canal when trying to come into the world. Other participants in the ritual assist the person through, by rubbing the legs and arms with care and lovingly guiding them through. A healing is performed at the end of the birthing phase for the person who has crawled across the star birthing blanket, a quilt that is handmade with a star design in a circular pattern. The person who is going through the healing is called from the other side by the grandfather and grandmother, who wait for the person to slowly reach them and then wash his or her face, hugging and cleansing the person with warm water. For some, part of the ceremony is a new drum that has just been made that has an umbilical cord (the loose tie end after the drum is wrapped) that is cut just as a baby's cord would be cut, as the drum is considered a baby. The drum is looked after just as a baby would be looked after. The piece of umbilical cord from the drum is tied in a cloth with tobacco and then the person going through the healing ceremony returns it to Mother Earth or keeps it. He or she now carries a new drum (Personal Experiences, 1990-2011).

- **Cedar Baths**—These are healing baths performed by a healer who heals people with the hands. The healer will use cedar water on the exposed parts of the body, such as the hands, face, and neck of the afflicted person, wiping away the stress and negative energies and illnesses that people carry. Following the ceremony, the water is returned to the earth and may become light to dark in color after the healing ceremony. The person who has received the healing will pray and pour the unclean water to the earth to have it return to positive energy. The healer is then able to tell the person what it was that was hurting, and why the person required healing. Sometimes, the healer will ask the subject to release the burden he or she has been carrying. Whatever it may be, healers carry the snake medicine that assists in removing negativity and sickness. The healer guides the person during the healing process (Personal Experiences, 1990-2011).

- **Dark Room Ceremonies**—These ceremonies are held in a dark room—nothing shiny, no lights, no candles, just in the dark—and can be held anywhere. They are usually conducted by a pipe carrier or medicine person who knows the ceremony. The conductor and participants will smoke the pipe, and then wait for answers, like a meditation when you go into a peaceful empty state of mind. A person may experience visions and obtain answers during this time (Personal Experiences, 1990-2011).

- **Funeral Ceremonies**—These are held to give the individual a traditional way of departing into the spirit world (*aadisookkaan*, or sacred in Ojibwe), for the sacred fire is burned for four days in honor of the person who has passed on. This ceremony is held in the Ojibwe Nation around the Sault Ste. Marie area (Personal Experiences, 1990-2011).

- **Ghost Dance**—"Ghost Dance" is the name usually applied to ceremonies in the religion of Jack Wilson, or "Wovoka," a Paiute prophet from Nevada who died in 1932. Jack led the circle dances through which Paiute opened themselves to spiritual influence. Moving always along the path of the sun—clockwise to the left—men, women, and children joined hands in a symbol of the community's living through the circle of the days. As they danced, they listened to Jack Wilson's songs celebrating the Almighty and his wondrous manifestations: the mountains, the clouds, snow, stars, trees, and antelope. Between dances, the people sat at Jack's feet, listening to him preach faith in universal love. The climax of Jack's personal growth came during a dramatic total eclipse of the sun on January 1, 1889 (Kehoe 1989, 5). In 1890, Wovoka, or Wilson, led a Ghost Dance and promised that all Indians who joined the Ghost Dance Faith (which spread quickly among the Cheyenne, Arapaho, Sioux, Kiowa, Caddo, and Paiute) would see the return of dead warriors and the decimated buffalo herds (Wilkins 2002, 215–216).

Today, two of the areas in which Ghost Dances are held are Montana in the United States and Manitoba, Canada. They are held in the fall, where feasts, dances, sweat lodges, healing, drumming, singing, teachings, and feasting the dead are practiced. The participants usually fast for four days during the ceremony.

- **Grandmother Moon Ceremony**—This is a ceremony held by women, but the Anishinaabe version of the ceremony permits men to attend in support of the women. It is a ceremony where women connect to Grandmother Moon, as women's menstrual cycles are referred to as moon time. The moon connects us with the water on the earth, and Mother Earth provides us with life. Women are life givers, and water surrounds the babies within their wombs. It is a time when women connect with one another, and connect with the Creator through drum, song, and prayer (Personal Experiences, 1990-2011).

- **Naming Ceremony**—This is performed in different ways. The Anishinaabe naming ritual involves a feast, sharing of gifts, and announcing one's name, clan, and colors. It is an important ceremony for the individual who is receiving his or her spiritual naming, as the ceremony acknowledges not only the people in attendance but also the four directions, spiritual entities, the participants, and the Creator. There are sometimes sponsors who attend for the individual who is being named. The individual being named will provide gifts to the sponsors and to the conductor(s) of the ceremony. Food for the feast is of significance in feasting the spirits, the Creator, and the people who attend.

The naming ceremony can be done inside a sweat lodge (Personal Experiences, 1990–2011).

- **Pipe Ceremonies**—These can be held alone with one pipe carrier or with more than one pipe carrier. Pipes (bawaagans) are used in prayer to seek information and guidance; they are smoked in sweat lodges, in sharing circles, in healing ceremonies, and in private. When smoking the sacred pipe, it is connecting to the Creator through prayer and acknowledging and giving thanks for all of creation. Pipe ceremonies are a part of the sun dance ceremony (Sun dance, August 2007) (Personal Experiences, 1990-2011).

The *Chanupa*, or Sacred Pipe, is considered by many Native peoples to be the single most sacred item used in a ceremony. It is used in many good ways, and its presence at a ceremony helps keep the ceremony focused. The Pipe Ceremonies hosted by Seven Circles[15] are similar to a "talking circle," where people are supported in speaking from their hearts. The ceremony leader helps maintain the sacredness within the space while the participants speak about their lives and community concerns. Once all participants have spoken, the Sacred Pipe is passed around so that everyone can "put their prayers into the pipe." Once the pipe is "loaded" with tobacco, the prayers are acknowledged, and the tobacco is smoked to release the prayers and set them in motion. A tobacco-less smoke mixture, *kinnickkinnick*, is used in this ceremony (Seven Circles Organization, 2007).

- **Powwows**—A powwow is a gathering of Native people who dance around an arbor that is covered with cedar, where the male drum groups, and sometimes female drum groups, sing and drum for the people who come to participate in the dance. It is a time when people of all ages come together to honor, respect, and dance for healing, praying, and blessings and to enrich their spirit and family connections. There is usually a sacred fire that burns where people go to offer prayers to the Creator.

When the powwow starts, there is a certain way people are to enter the powwow arena. Usually the veterans come in first, carrying eagle staffs and flags; then the head dancers come in, followed by the royalty. Men dancers usually enter before women dancers: The men's traditional northern

---

15   The Seven Circles Foundation, based in California, is an educational organization established to promote and support spiritual practices based on the ancient ways of Native American Indigenous People. The Foundation brings these practices to the community at large to improve the quality of life for all.

and southern grass and fancy dancers are usually followed by the women's traditional northern and southern jingle and fancy dancers. The teen categories then enter in the same order, and last of all come the tiny tots. After all the dancers have entered the powwow arena, there is a veterans' song, a flag song, and an invocation by a respected elder from the community. This is usually followed by an introduction of all the royalty from visiting reservations and communities. There are two different types of dancing powwows. One is the traditional powwow, where there's just social dancing, and the other is a contest powwow, where dancers and singers compete for money. Dancers are judged on how they dance and the rhythm they keep with the drums. Each category has different songs that they dance to, such as the ladies' side step for the jingle dress[16] (Mille Lacs Ojibwe, 2007).

The powwow is possibly the most important community ritual on the Plains. Viewing the powwow in its ritual and symbolic dimensions reveals the wide range of ways the powwow affects individuals and communities and allows them to act on their social and cultural world. As culturally and socially standardized and repetitive action wrapped in a web of symbolism, ritual—having both cognitive and emotional affects—builds individuals' confidence in themselves, in others, and in their local tribal community (Lassiter 2005, 68).

- **Sacred** means something special, something out of the ordinary, and often it concerns a very personal part of each one of us because it describes our dreams, our changing, and our personal ways of seeing the world. The sacred is also something that is shared, and this sharing or collective experience is necessary in order to keep the oral traditions and sacred ways vital (Beck et al. 1992, 6).

- **Sacredness** is depicted through the standing rock sun dance site; some medicine men say that sites where sun dances are held are marked forever as locations where sacred things have happened. Some of the people at Standing Rock have told me that traces of a sun dance done by Sitting Bull when he was in Canada still remain after nearly 125 years. They say the holes where the poles were set in the ground, as well as the location of the altar,

---

16 Jingle dress dancers are female dancers of different ages, from the very young to adults. They wear regalia that have many metal jingle cones, tiers of seven rows attached to their regalia that jingle when they dance. They dance for healing. Gifts are given to the jingle dress dancers from the Creator.

can be plainly seen, because nothing has grown there during the intervening time (Deloria, 2006).

- **Seven Grandfather Teachings** are wisdom, love, respect, courage, honesty, humility, and truth.

- **Shaky Tent Ceremony**—This is a traditional Anishinaabe ceremony performed by the conductor Theon, who has been gifted to perform this ceremony. Theon is able to provide spiritual information to individuals for medicine, and for those seeking knowledge on their path, dreams, and visions. The conductor sits inside a special type of tent, which is put up with seven poles symbolic of the seven ancient spirits. The tent is covered half with blue cloth and half with red cloth, and the conductor sits inside the tent, where he converses with ancient spirits. Prior to the start of the ceremony, the conductor explains his purpose in doing the shaky tent, and why he has to perform this ceremony for the people. He will move inside the tent, and the room where the tent is placed is darkened. He will then invite the spirits to be there and the shaky tent will start shaking back and forth. The Native languages can be heard as things transpire inside the tent. Individuals seeking information will pass the conductor tobacco and ask their questions, and then the tent will begin to shake, quite forcefully. The sound of bells ringing will stop when the shaking is finished. It is then time for the conductor to speak with the individual who has asked for information. The spiritual connection is made; the spirits know who is asking the questions. They can see the questioner, and understand, for instance, the health problems, or dreams and visions about which the questioner is seeking help, and they are able to interpret them. They may even offer directions to take specific medicines for healing (Personal Experiences, 1990-2011).

- **Talking Circles**—Talking circles with talking sticks (to allow all participants persons the power to express themselves) have been used in some American Indian groups as a strategy for dealing with many problems, from alcoholism to chronic illnesses such as diabetes and cancer. Often, when someone is diagnosed with a chronic illness, issues of self-image, identity, and coping figure significantly. Talking circles provide an excellent opportunity to encourage discussion about some difficult emotions and meet with others who are facing the same challenges (Trafzer 2001, 176).

- **Third Eye Ceremony**—This ceremony is performed by Theon, the conductor of the Shaky Tent, who knows the ceremony from the ancient ways. Theon uses fish oil to perform the opening of the third eye, which is in the area above our two eye sockets, in the middle; it is where we can see spiritually. This ceremony is to help that eye to be active and clear, and to not be closed off (Personal Experiences, 1990-2011).

- **Sun Dance Ceremony**—This is a sacred dance once performed annually by Siouan-speaking tribesmen in which men put skewers through their flesh and danced until the flesh broke. This was the most supreme offering that could possibly be made to spirits (Wolfson 1993, 77). Women and men still dance in the sun dance, along with young children. Today, many other tribal people, such as the Anishinaabe, participate in the sun dance. The sun dance ceremony is an act of sacrifice for prayer for the people. It is a cleansing within oneself, a spiritual journey. Prayer and dance, drum and song are all part of the healing. Native people carry medicines, pipes, and sacred items; have dreams and vision quests; participate in fasting; and connect to the spirit world—actions that are all part of this healing ceremony (Pipestone sun dance, August 2–5, 2007).

- **Sunrise Ceremony**—This ceremony is performed as the sun is rising, to greet Grandfather Sun and give thanks for the rising sun and what it provides for us, and to give thanks to the Creator for all of creation. Prayers and pipes are smoked by the conductor(s) of the ceremony. This ceremony is performed at sacred fire arbors, and the morning is greeted anywhere that you wish to offer and greet the day in prayer (Personal Experiences, 1990-2011).

- **Sweat Lodge Ceremony**—The Anishinaabe lodge is erected by tying together long willow tree branches into a dome-shaped frame with an eastern door entrance. A sacred fire is ignited within feet of the lodge prior to the sweat lodge ceremony to heat the stones. The sacred fire is surrounded by a mound of soil in the shape of a crescent moon piled up in behind and around the fire and stones, a cedar trail surrounds the perimeter of the fire with a trail of cedar that has been hand cut by the women and trails into the lodge at the entrance of the eastern door. The sacred fire is ignited by the fire keeper with his flint, and grandmothers and grandfathers (rocks) are heated under the fire wood and are heated in preparation for putting them into the centre of the lodge. There is a circular hole inside the lodge that has been dug up to place the heated stones in the hole in Mother Earth. The lodge is symbolic of the womb, and the womb is symbolic of Mother Earth. Long wide canvas is placed over and around the frame of the lodge to allow for total darkness. Tobacco is given to the conductor of the ceremony in exchange for whatever participants are asking for. They may ask for a name, or if they are hurting in certain parts of their bodies, they will ask for prayers. The conductor will direct everyone to the place in the lodge where he feels they need to be. Lodges can be for women or men separately, or they can be mixed lodges, with women on one side and men on the other. The conductor asks the fire keeper to smudge everyone, usually with sage. Sweat lodge ceremonies have several rounds. Once everyone is inside the lodge, the first round begins. Seven grandfathers are brought in if it is a naming ceremony, and nine will be brought in for the nine months in the womb. If asking for grandmother spirits, the number is thirteen. Any extra helpers come after. Once in the lodge, the conductor feels out what comes to him; he then lets it take place. He may have songs sung with drumming and rattles to invite the spirits into the lodge. At the second round, the southern door is called upon to release whatever is bothering you in life. This is called the sharing round. Stress causes sickness, which is why we do the sharing round. After everyone shares, then comes the supporting round. The western door is opened to allow for more grandfathers and grandmothers (stones) to be brought in, and then the door is closed. The conductor will give support when the spirits bring messages. The door is then opened again, and more grandfathers and grandmothers are brought in; this is the thank-you round. Prayers are given for the people in the hospital and people who are sick and cannot make it; we think about them and send them energy from the lodge. The door is opened by everyone saying, "All my relations." The sacred pipe is smoked to give thanks before the feast. We feast at the last door; food offerings include wild meat or fish, corn, berries, and candy and are shared and offered to the spirits; the food is put into the sacred fire. Everybody goes out, hugs are shared outside by the fire, and tobacco is offered to the fire in thanks. Following the sweat lodge, everyone then enters in the main lodge to feast. The length of time for this ceremony depends on the number of people who are participating and the time it takes for sharing, singing, and the drumming to take place. This sweat lodge usually starts at around 6:30 p.m. and can run late into the night (Leonard's Interview/Participant Observations, July 2007).

- **Teaching Lodge**—The teaching lodge is where Native people gather to speak of oral traditions, storytelling, and traditional teachings. People gather in a circle, where prayers and ceremonies are held for the purpose of learning and uniting in the traditional ways of life (Personal Experiences, 1990-2011).

- **Yuwipi Ceremony**—In the yuwipi, the practitioner is firmly bound up with ropes: Each finger is tied with knots, the hands are firmly tied, and often the feet are tied in a similar manner. Blankets—or in the old days, buffalo robes—are wrapped around him very tightly, and bound with ropes, the man is placed on the floor, or preferably the ground, and the tipi or lodge is sealed so that total darkness prevails. Around the room are distributed a large number (usually 405) of very small pouches of tobacco wrapped in red cloth—gifts to the spirits that will come and participate in the ritual, healing and answering questions. The practitioner begins to sing his yuwipi power songs, and soon the blue sparks of the spirits are seen coming into the room or tent. People attending the ceremony feel the brush of bird wings; sometimes, they hear the patter of animal feet; sometimes, they feel a great wind that, strangely, does not disturb anything; and frequently, they hear animal noises or strange languages used by the spirits attending the practitioner. In this state, the practitioner can heal people, find lost objects, and predict the future. The minds of everyone attending are clearly read by the practitioner, and messages are passed back and forth between him and the spirits. Sometimes, there is a long silence as the practitioner goes to other times and places and gathers information needed by someone in the group. During this time, it is necessary for the people to pray for the return of the medicine man, since his soul has left his body and has gone to search for answers (Deloria 2006, 84).

- **Windego Ceremony**—The contrary people, the clowns who have special powers, participate in ceremonies that are held in the winter, opposite the summer and fall ceremonies. They carry the spirit of the *windego*, a spiritual being, and participate as healers at the ceremony. This particular ceremony is held within the

Anishinaabe nation. The clowns are allies and friends to ordinary people, and sometimes mock the practitioners by dancing behind the dancers and mocking their steps, interrupting speeches by dance leaders as the clowns did in the aboriginal winter ceremony, and mimicking shamans in their work. The clowns serve to neutralize excesses, to return them to a balanced state. Clowns are also considered to be powerful in their own way, and different from ordinary people (Beck 1992, 311).

The Big Drum and Sun Dance Ceremony Images

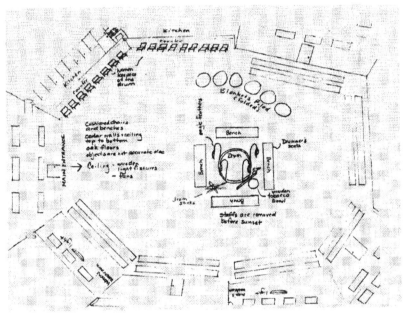

Big Drum Ceremony Drawing – Inside the Mille Lacs Band of Ojibwe Ceremonial Building

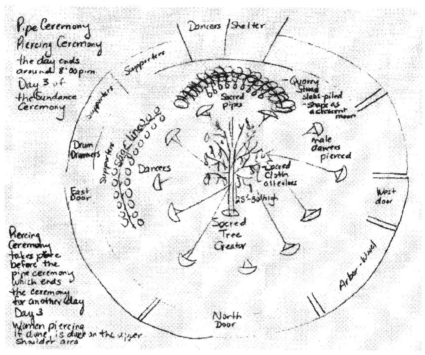

Sun Dance—Sacred Grounds—Pipestone, Minnesota

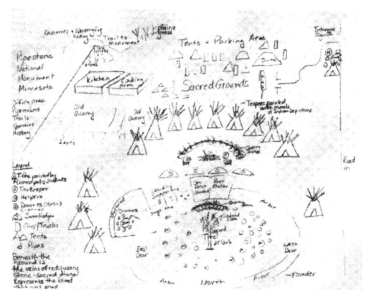

Sun Dance Ceremony—Piercing and Pipe Ceremony

Pipestone National Monument Map

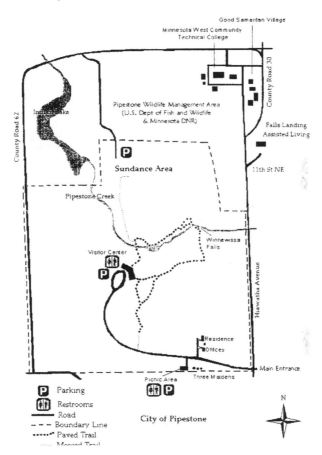

Pipestone Monument Map

Glossary

Anishinaabe, Chippewa, Ojibwe: The "original people." A woodland tribe who lived west of the Great Lakes in Canada, Michigan, Minnesota, and Wisconsin.

attending ceremony: Participating in traditional Native ceremonies for praying, rituals, and well-being with family and friends.

Buddhism: Eastern religion: a world religion or philosophy based on the teaching of the Buddha and holding that a state of enlightenment can be attained by suppressing worldly desires.

Cherokee: *Ani-Yun'wiya* meaning leading or principal people. They are Southeastern tribes who lived in northern Georgia, eastern Tennessee, and western North Carolina.

clan: Spirit animal that is given to an individual, which tells them what type of spiritual beings help them on their paths and walk with them on their journey.

colors: Each person has specific colors that are given to them by the Creator.

Dakota: The largest tribe of Siouan-speaking Native Americans, who lived in Minnesota and Wisconsin.

Daoism: Refers to an indigenous Chinese religious tradition(s). Daoists (Taoists) understand the Dao as source of all that is unnamable mystery, all-pervading numinousness and the cosmological process which is the universe.

dodem: Ojibwe word for clan.

fire keeper: A man who carries a flint to light a sacred fire and also tends to the fire for ceremony and gatherings.

Gusala: The Grandfather, the Great Unknown, the spirits.

Ho Chunk: North American tribe of Siouan language family called the

Winnebago, who have traditional culture, religious, and social traits resembling those of the Siouan-speaking tribes of the Great Plains. The tribe's economy and daily life were similar to those of the Northeast hunters and trappers.

Islam—one of the three major world religions, along with Judaism and Christianity, that profess monotheism, or the belief in a single God.

Judaism: A religion developed among the ancient Hebrews and characterized by a belief in one transcendent God who has revealed himself to Abraham, Moses, and the Hebrew prophets and by a religious life in accordance with Scriptures and rabbinical traditions.

Lakota: A member of a western division of the Dakota people.

medicine bundle: A soft bag made from animal skin, which holds sacred objects. Today, medicine bags are made from different materials and hold sacred objects and medicines.

Medicine Wheel: A symbol that helps us see things holistically in all aspects of life, within our spiritual, emotional, physical, and mental well-being.

Methodist: Founded by John Wesley, who was ordained a deacon in 1725, and admitted to the priesthood of the Church of England in 1728. A holy club was formed in which the club members adhered strictly and methodically to religious precepts and practices, visiting prisons and comforting the sick. Schoolmates called them "Methodist" because of their adherence to methods. The religion is still practiced today.

Mohawk: Native North American tribe of the Iroquoian language family and of the Northeast culture area, a Six Nations tribe.

Native culture: The integrated pattern of human knowledge, belief, and behavior that depends upon the capacity for learning and transmitting knowledge to succeeding generations.

pipe carrier: A man or woman who carries the sacred artifact (pipe) that is smoked with tobacco or kinnickkinnick in prayer for spiritual help and guidance.

Pipestone Quarry: A site in Pipestone, Minnesota, where Native Americans quarry a hard, reddish, claylike stone used to make sacred pipes. The stone is sacred.

sacred fire: A fire that is ignited by a fire keeper with a flint and burns during ceremonies, such as sweat lodges, sharing circles, pipe ceremonies, funerals, and fasting. It is a means of contact with the Creator and the spirit world through prayer. The fire provides spiritual connections, comfort, and blessings.

spirit dishes: Food that is traditional in nature, such as berries, fish, corn, wild game and rice for the ceremonial participants and spirits, and candy that is used for the little-people spirits. Spirit dishes can be prepared for the spirits of your ancestors, and consist of food they enjoyed when they were alive.

spirit name: A spiritual name passed through a spiritual person from the Creator to the person asking for the name. Babies can be given their spirit names at birth.

sweat lodge conductor: A man or woman who holds a position at the main door to the sweat lodge and carries the knowledge to conduct the sweat lodge ceremony.

Windego Ceremony: A healing ceremony for the contrary (clown) people who participate as healers of the people.

Wounded Knee: An unincorporated community in South Dakota that is on the Pine Ridge Indian Reservation. Wounded Knee was the site of two conflicts between the local Native American population and the United States government. In the late 1880s, the Sioux began practicing a religion taught by Wovoka, a Paiute prophet who promised that performing the ritual ghost dance would result in the return of native lands, the rise of dead ancestors, the disappearance of the whites, and a future of eternal peace and prosperity. Nearby white settlers were frightened by the rituals and called for federal intervention. The US Army believed Chief Sitting Bull to be the instigator of an impending rebellion, and he was arrested in December 1890. As he was being led away over the objections of his supporters, a gunfight erupted. Thirteen people, including Sitting Bull, were killed. His followers then fled, some to the camp of Chief Big Foot. The Seventh Cavalry pursued the Sioux to an encampment near Wounded Knee Creek. On December 29, 1890, a shot was fired within the camp, and the army began shooting. Accounts of the precise events and the death toll vary considerably, but it is likely that the soldiers killed between 150 and 370 Sioux men, women, and children, the great majority of whom were unarmed bystanders. Thirty-one US soldiers were killed in action, many of them from fire from their own troops.

The second incident started on February 27, 1973, when armed supporters of the American Indian Movement (AIM) seized and held Wounded Knee, demanding a US Senate investigation of Native American problems. Federal law enforcement officers were sent to the site, and during gunfire exchanges, two Native Americans were killed and several people on both sides were injured. The siege ended seventy-one days later, when the Native Americans were promised that negotiations concerning their grievances would be considered. After one meeting with White House representatives and a promise of a second one, the Native Americans were informed that their treaty grievances should be referred to Congress. No further meetings took place.

Bibliography

"Aboriginal Healing Foundation." Aboriginal Healing Foundation website, April 2011. Retrieved from www.ahf.ca.

Ableidinger, Sister Marianna. *Integrating Ojibwe Native American and Roman Catholic Spiritualities.* Minnesota: Saint Mary's University of Minnesota, 2000.

Arden, Harvey. *Wisdomkeepers: Meetings with Native American Spiritual Elders.* Hillsboro, OR: Beyond Words Publishing, 1990.

Beck, Peggy V., Anna Lee Walters, and Nia Francisco, *The Sacred, Ways of Knowledge, Sources of Life.* Tsaile, AZ: Navajo Community College Press, 1988.

Biolsi, Thomas, ed. *A Companion to the Anthropology of American Indians.* Malden, MA: Blackwell Publishing, 2008

"Culture and Traditions." Mille Lacs Band of Ojibwe. Retrieved April 2007 from http://www.millelacsband.com/Page_Culture1.aspx.

Deloria, Vine Jr. *The World We Used to Live In, Remembering the Powers of the Medicine Men.* Golden, CO: Fulcrum Publishing, 2006.

Eadie, Betty J. *Embraced by the Light.* Placerville, CA: Gold Leaf Press, 1992.

Edmunds, R. David, Frederick E. Hoxie, and Neal Salisbury. *The People, A History of Native America, Vol. 1 and Vol. 2.* Boston, MA: Houghton Mifflin, 2007.

Hollihan, Tony. *Great Chiefs.* Edmonton, AB: Folklore Publishing, 2002.

Kehoe, Alice Beck. *The Ghost Dance: Ethnohistory and Revitalization.* Orlando, FL: Saunders College Publishing, 1989.

Lassiter, Luke E. *Invitation to Anthropology.* Lanham, MD: AltaMira, 2002.

Lassiter, Luke E. *The Power of the Kiowa Song.* Sierra Vista, AZ: University of Arizona Press. Arizona, 1998.

Lassiter, Luke E. *Powwow*. Lincoln, NE: University of Nebraska, 2005. *Unrepentent: Kevin Annett and Canada's Genocide* documentary. DVD video. Directed by Louie Lawless and written by Kevin Daniel Annett, narrator and producer Lori O'Rorke. Annett-Lawless Copyright. British Columbia, 2007. Retrieved May 9, 2011 from ttp://www.worldcat.org/title/unrepentant-kevin-annett-and-canadas-genocide/oclc/123759580. Retrieved April 8, 2011. http://topdocumentaryfilms.com/unrepentant-kevin-annett-canadas-genocide, 2006.

"Seven Circles' Pipe Ceremonies." Seven Circles Foundation website. Retrieved May 17, 2007 from http://www.sevencircles.org/pipe.

Starita, Joe. *The Dull Knifes of Pine Ridge: A Lakota Odyssey*. Lincoln, NE: University of Nebraska Press, 1996.

Stevenson, Mary. *Footprints in the Sand*. Retrieved April 25, 2011. 1984 (1936) http://www.footprints-inthe-sand.com/.

Sturtevant, W.C. *Native North American Spirituality of the Eastern Woodlands: Sacred Myths, Dreams, Visions, Speeches, Healing Formulas, Rituals, and Ceremonials*. New York: Paulist Press, 1979.

Trafzer, Clifford E. and Diane Weiner, eds. *Medicine Ways, Disease, Health, and Survival among Native Americans*. Lanham, MD: AltaMira, 2001.

Wilkins, David E. *American Indian Politics and the American Political System*. Lanham, MD: Rowman and Littlefield Publishers, 2002.

Wolfson, Evelyn. *From the Earth to Beyond the Sky*. Boston: Houghton Mifflin, 1993.

Part 2:
Integrating Traditional Medicine
& Healers into Western Clinics

Traditional Indian Medicine and Western Medicine
A Comparision of Values

Traditional Indian Medicine	Western Medicine
- Integrated, holistic approach to health: body, mind and spirit interact together to form person	- Analytic approach: separation of body, mind, and spirit (total split between medicine and religion)
- Emphasis on prevention of sickness	- Emphasis on disease, treatment
- Personal responsibility for health and sickness	- Impersonal, "scientific" approach to health and sickness
- Health and sickness understood in terms of the laws of nature	- Health and sickness understood in terms of quantifiable, scientific data
- Man living in balance with nature, and natural law	- Man controlling nature, manipulating natural variables
- Traditional medicine governed by the laws of the Creation: everything we need comes from the Earth ~ Our food, medicines, water, education, religion, and laws	- Western medicine governed by the laws of the State, man-made laws which grow out of a political-economic system
- Medicine man is accountable to the Creator, to the people, to the Elders of his medicine society	- Doctor is accountable to the government and to his professional association
- Medicine is not for sale, not for profit ~ it is a gift to be shared	- Medicine is business, the patient is the consumer, the doctor and the medical industry profit
- The land and the people support the medicine man and his practice	- The government, the taxpayer and the consumer support the doctor and the practice of medicine
- Encourages self-sufficiency, self-care and responsibility and control by the people	- Encourages dependency and abdication of self-government by the people

Garden River First Nation Wellness Centre Placard

Preface

This study uses theory that is the core of anthropology and reflects on the qualitative and quantitative methods that provide realistic goals and objectives for the purpose of integrating traditional medicine and healers into Western clinics in order to assist the health of First Nations' peoples.

In defining theory, questions are asked in order to sort out the information that anthropologists collect. A solid understanding of the history and theory of Aboriginal peoples remains a collection of exotic ethnography, if applied research is not put into practice to benefit humanity.

The anthropological approach is to convey transparent meanings and cultural viewpoints on how traditional healers are gifted to heal as helpers to the Creator, and how the integration will benefit First Nations peoples for generations to come. The study reflects on the Anishinaabe approach to storytelling, and on how information is traditionally passed on.

The pedagogy of traditional methods of healing , and the reasons behind the applied health and cultural research that is necessary to provide the foundation, are reviewed in the study in order to build from historical and cultural influences that deter the restoration of traditional and cultural practices of First Nations peoples.

The following research study will draw on the ethnographic data, cross-cultural comparisons, traditional and Western methods, storytelling, key contributors, traditional healing roles, health information, global perspectives, ethnoscientists, and the findings and recommendations that provide a foundation to pursue further applied research, and activities in which to integrate healers into Western clinics.

Acknowledgments

Without the support and approval of the North Shore Tribal Council Health Centre's Health Director and Health Professionals, the traditional healers and clients of healers across the North Shore, the Batchewana First Nations' Chief and Council, the Health Centre Staff; the Garden River First Nations' Chief and Council and administration and health staff; and the Sault Ste. Marie Indian Friendship Centre's Executive Director and Staff, this applied research project would not be possible.

I am grateful for the support you, the participants, provided, and the qualitative reflections and vital information you contributed toward the project. You have provided your information with honesty and integrity, with a holistic view toward "integrating traditional medicine and healers into Western clinics," which you wholeheartedly believe will assist indigenous peoples with their health issues. You have given unconditionally to benefit people.

My gratitude goes out to all my professors at the University of North Texas who supported me throughout my studies and research. Your knowledge, dedication, and support are graciously appreciated during my time as a graduate student of UNT in the Public Affairs and Community Service Applied Anthropology program, from which I obtained my Master of Science degree.

Introduction

The North Shore Tribal Council (NSTC)—Mamaweswen, N'Mninoeyaa (I am fine) Aboriginal Health Access Centre includes the partner First Nations: Batchewana First Nation, Garden River First Nation, Thessalon First Nation, Mississauga First Nation, Serpent River First Nation, Sagamok Anishnawbek, and Atikameksheng First Nation including the Sault Ste. Marie Indian Friendship Centre.

History and Background

The Health Access Centre located in Cutler, Ontario, Canada, is the key sponsor contact for this project. The Centre, developed in 1995, receives provincial funding through the Aboriginal Healing and Wellness Strategy. The services delivered under this agreement are based on the outreach model, discussed below, to each of the Seven (7) First Nations and the Indian Friendship Centre in Sault Ste. Marie.

The Aboriginal Health Access program mandate is to:

- improve accessibility, comprehensiveness, coordination, continuity and accountability of primary health care programs and services;

- respond to community-identified health priorities with effective, culturally sensitive and accessible primary health care programs;

- reflect the importance of disease prevention and health promotion in the planning and implementation of primary health care programs;

- increase client participation in their health care;

- ensure client access to Traditional Healers/Elders for those who request such services and to other Traditional Healing/ Health activities (2008/2009 Annual Report NSTC).

The programs include the Minomodzawin Diabetes Education Program; Fetal Alcohol Spectrum Disorder/Child Nutrition Program; Long Term Care and Aging at Home Program(s); N'Mninoeyaa Aboriginal Mental Health Services; Regional Traditional Health Program, and the Information Technology Program—Health. This Centre is similar to provincially funded Community Health Centres that have a mandate to provide primary health care to those who face barriers to access. The North Shore Tribal Council has focused on diagnosis and treatment of illness to compliment the existing health promotion, illness and injury prevention programs delivered and controlled by the First Nations (2008/2009 NSTC Annual Report).

The Research Goal

The major goal of this research is to investigate the incorporation of traditional medicine and healers into the Western Centre, N'Mninoeyaa Aboriginal Health Access Centre, in order to enhance health service delivery and improve the health of Native people.

Specific Research Goals in the North Shore Tribal Council (NSTC) area include:

1. to investigate the major health problems facing Native people
2. to investigate the role that traditional healing may play (or could play) in overcoming these health problems
3. to identify the factors that deter the integration of traditional medicine/healers with biomedicine (either within or outside the centre)
4. to investigate and recommend strategies to increase access to traditional healers within the NSTC catchment area

Context of Work
The World Health Organization (WHO) and Integration

The World Health Organization (WHO) encapsulates within their definition of health of a holistic approach to health practiced by traditional societies as "a state of complete physical, mental, and social well-being and not merely an absence of disease or infirmity," and to achieve this healthy state, the patient must feel comfortable with the system providing the care. Therapy must have cultural relevance in any system; as a belief system identifies a specific cause of illness, the cure must be sought within that belief system, and healers must be aware of the patient's understanding of the illness (Wheatley 1990, 217–220).

The World Health Organization is encouraging an integration of traditional medicine (TM) into healthcare systems worldwide. The holistic approach to health practiced by traditional societies is represented by seventy countries that met to discuss how to make these medicines more available and noted a need for more research. Traditional medicine covers a wide variety of therapies and practices, which vary from country to country and region to region. Some countries use traditional medicine and reference it as "alternative" or "complementary" medicine (CAM). Traditional medicine has been used for thousands of years with great contributions made by practitioners to human health, particularly as primary health care providers at the community level. TM/CAM has maintained its popularity worldwide. Since the 1990s its use has surged in many developed and developing countries (Sommers 2009, 36).

In order to integrate American Indians into the national health care policies and programs, the WHO recommends that traditional health care merge with modern health care. The First Nations cultural focus on health is similar to the WHO's. The WHO is not looking merely at the absence of disease or infirmity but at the physical, mental, and social well-being of populations. First Nations cultural focus is on the Medicine Wheel teachings that include the four directions—north, south, west, and east. Within these four directions are the physical, emotional (social), mental, and spiritual well-being of their members, constituting a holistic approach (Ramsey and Beesley 2006, 90). American Indian culture has a strong link between medicine and religion, while modern medicine has a view of human health relative to the physical laws of science. American Indians view spirit as the life force, and spiritual health is inextricably tied to physical health. The patient's spirituality is one contributor to an effective clinician-patient relationship. The patient's perception of the level of spirituality plays a role in how effective the healer can be. American Indians have a belief in a synergy and a connectedness at some level between Mother Earth/nature, Father Sky, and all life through the Creator, Great Spirit, Great Mystery, or Maker of All Things. One must follow the prescribed life ways to maintain optimal mental, physical, and spiritual health. American Indians have a belief that all things have life and spirit, and are intricately related in the universe. Traditional healers help to restore balance through prayer, chants, and smudging (a ritual that utilizes the smoke from burning sacred herbs to cleanse the negative energies around a person). Herbal remedies include salves, herbs, tobacco, ointments, teas, and dances. Therapeutic touch, energy work, massage, and acupressure are used (Broome and Broome 2007, 161–173).

A Global Perspective on
Traditional Healing

The following countries provide a global perspective on traditional medicines and the modalities that healers use. Included are the cross-cultural comparisons that are important to understanding alternative medicines.

Australia

Ancient Aboriginal medicine is finding a foothold in the fast-paced world of the city workplace. The *Ngangkari*, Aboriginal medicine men, work as a team to administer the healing power of touch. Mystical medicine has joined a panoply of alternative treatments sought by a troubled world. The medicine men's touch is not gentle; after probing, they firmly grip by their fingernails the flesh and pull it hard, capturing what is to us invisible mystery; it is a black clot. The clot is like a stone, a block to health, and a wellspring of illness. The medicine men expel air in their hands. They puff their hands, snap, and cast the troublesome "stone" out the window. A soothing rub and healing-over motion is done after the "stone" is removed. They zero in on a chronic area. The Ngangkari touch a spot in the low back of their subject. They locate his spirit, as it has moved. They are unclear why it has moved, but it belongs below the rib cage at the front. They check his blood flow by tracing his veins. It is good, and he is cleansed and repaired. The Ngangkari give instructions not to drink anything hot or the spirit may jump back. The patient also needs to stay away from alcohol, as he or she may not feel different right away. It may take a couple of weeks. The Ngangkari charge $50 for one treatment, or $200 for the spiritual purging of houses where inhabitants are troubled by bad spirits called mumbles. The ability to deal with spirits is of profound importance.

They attend to patients in hospitals, at home, and at the worker's office. They see ten people a day. The demand is overwhelming. Cheryl Newman, a subject who receives treatments, says, "I had bad neck and shoulder pain, but I see them regularly and they make me feel good. It's a cleansing feeling. There is something there, something unusual." The Ngangkari medicine men are well known and used regularly for healing (Harris 2009, 1–3).

In Australia, there is a small clinic in a fibro-cement building where a nurse is based. Her attention to sickness derives from training in, and delivery of, a largely Western biomedical approach to illness and disease. Local church leaders provide prayer and holy oil, and the local healers, or *maparn*, men or women, respond to people's sickness using a traditionalist model of diagnosis and healing. In the home of a sick woman, many gather around her unconscious body, as nurses, church leaders, and maparn provide care and attention, attempting to save her life. The nurse maintains the drip, the church leaders pray, and the maparn works to remove the sickness from her body. The woman stirs after a period of time and sits up on her bed after being in a diabetic coma, and, oblivious to the surrounding people, asks for something to eat (McCoy 2008, 226–227).

United States

In California, a hospital welcomes Hmong shamans to perform ceremonies and chants. One patient works with a Hmong medicine man on his diabetes and hypertension. Mr. Lee is the Hmong shaman who begins a healing process by looping a coiled thread around the patient's wrist, summoning the ailing man's runaway soul. Mr. Lee encircles the patient in an invisible "protective shield," traced in the air with his finger. Mr. Lee says, "The soul is the shaman's responsibility." The Mercy Medical Centre located in Merced has Hmong patients from northern Laos, where healing includes IV drips, syringes, and blood glucose monitors. The Hmong rely on their spiritual beliefs to get them through illnesses. The hospital has a Hmong shaman policy, the country's first, that formally recognizes the cultural role of traditional healers like Mr. Lee, inviting them to perform nine approved ceremonies in the hospital, including "soul calling" and chanting in a voice not to exceed three decibels (Brown 2009, 1).

Philippines

The implications of practice and research are found in the Philippines, where Dr. Nelia Maramba combines the rigorous discipline of science with an open mind to traditional medicines. Dr. Maramba is the overall coordinator of the National Integrated Research Program for Medicinal Plants

(NIRPROMP). She says, "We have been a lead country in herbal medicine" (Jorge 2009, 1). NIRPROMP has always advocated evidence-based scientific study to validate efficacy, safety, and quality of control of herbal medicine preparations, and adherence to the WHO guidelines on herbal medicines (1993). Four approved medicines on the Philippine National Drug Formulary were researched under the National Science and Technology Authority, now called the Department of Science and Technology (1987). The NIRPROMP found solutions to the most common problems, such as cough (lagundi), pain (yerba buena), renal stones (sambong), diarrhea (bayabas), intestinal worms (niyog-niyogan), high blood pressure (bawang), high blood sugar (ampalaya), fungal infections (akapulko), tooth decay (tsaang gubat), and arthritis and gout (ulasimang bato or pansit-pansitan). The first mission of the organization concerns finding symptoms, and this is complete. Mission two is to find cures for the symptoms. Five herbal medicines are included in the Philippines National Drug Formulary of 2009. A prescriptive form, such as a tablet, syrup, and ointment, has been developed. Medicines are more affordable, and farmers are growing lagundi, sambong, yerba buena, and other traditional remedies. The pharmaceutical conglomerates are faced with competition from herbal medicines locally sourced and manufactured; they have offered the Philippines $15 million to give them all the rights, all the intellectual property rights from the beginning. The local manufacturers have refused. As Dr. Maramba says, "Why would you sell your own country?" During her studies abroad in Georgia in the United States, her pharmacology professor asserted, "There will be a time when one's mind cannot anymore formulate new synthetic medicine, but God is always there in his creation, and the active principles created by God will be the one to save mankind." Dr. Nelia Maramba and the National Integrated Research Program of Medicinal Plants continue their advances in Filipino herbal medicines, reaching far beyond the ten most common diseases, such as TB, the flu, and drug-resistant staphylococcal infection (Jorge 2009, 1–3).

Complementary and Alternative Medicine (CAM)

Many countries utilize CAM methods for their health, and do not necessarily have a full grasp of traditional Native medicine. The widespread use of CAM in many countries in Europe, including the United Kingdom, Denmark, Germany, and France, and other countries, such as Australia, New Zealand, China, African countries, Canada, the United States and Mexico in North America, and Central and South American countries practice CAM/TM. There are over seventy countries that utilize CAM/TM as alternative ways of healing for their illnesses. CAM therapies are called holistic, natural, alternative, or complementary therapies, and include a large number of available treatments. The treatments include acupuncture, herbal medicine, naturopathy, nutritional therapy, homeopathy, Ayurveda, traditional Chinese medicine, and hypnotherapy. Spiritual healing methods include chiropractic treatments, osteopathy, Alexandra techniques, reiki, touch of health, aura soma, bioelectromagnetic therapies, aromatherapy, massage, flower essences, rebirthing, Maori medicine, and yoga, meditation, and Chelation therapies. The best way to find a reliable practitioner is by word of mouth. When visiting holistic practitioners, request to see their relevant qualifications and ask about what experience they have had treating people with your particular health issue. Most modalities have national associations that oversee practitioner qualifications (NZPAME 2009, 2–7).

UK citizens use alternative practitioners at a rate of five to six times that of medical doctors. Studies show that 90 percent of the population in the United Kingdom has used at least one form of complementary therapy. In Denmark, 24 percent of the people use complementary therapy that is reimbursed, and 49 percent of the population in France use CAM therapy. The factor that drives global CAM trends is the lack of side effects from such treatments. Practitioners look to treat the whole person rather than just the symptoms, and therapies empower patients by encouraging them to participate and take control over their own health issues. In 2002, a New Zealand Health Survey found that 12 percent of adults were referred to complementary health practitioners by their general practitioners. The most common reason for referring patients to CAM practitioners was "failure of conventional medicine." An "integrative medicine approach" should integrate the best available health treatments from orthodox and natural medicine says Phillip Cottingham, who is a thirty-year veteran of the natural health industry, and founder of a training institute, Wellpark College of Natural Therapies. Most open-minded doctors who refer patients to CAM are happy with the outcome. In Germany, 58 percent of general practitioners in a 1993 study preferred complementary to orthodox medicine. A survey of nursing practitioners (NPs) showed that 80 percent used CAM therapies and had undergone training in such therapies, and 92 percent of the NPs who had not used CAM therapies were prepared to do so. Regardless of the constant criticism, 65 percent of hospital doctors believe CAM therapies have a place in mainstream medicine. The British Medical Association states that there is a place for CAM therapies in health care as long as doctors retain overall control of the treatments their patients receive. In the United States, alternative medicine electives are offered in more than two dozen medical schools. The treatments vary and include everything from acupuncture to spiritual healing (NZPAME 2009, 1–7; NCCAM 2010; CAM 2010).

FIRST NATIONS HEALTH AND POLITICAL INFLUENCES

There are trials and tribulations whenever First Nations are subjected to colonialist's practices, which continue to be at the forefront of political engagements with First Nations. Many factors come into play when there is a political struggle to obtain funding to enable healthy, sustainable, and viable communities. The political information highlight the First Nations' political struggles.

The Indian Health Transfer Policy

The Indian Health Transfer Policy was approved by Health Canada in 1988 (Jacklin and Warry, 217). The goals and objectives of the initiative are to enhance Aboriginal self-determination in health care by providing First Nations with increased control over the design, delivery, and administration of health services. The Health Transfer Policy recognizes the need for self-determination in health care and represents a movement toward self-government. When the critical medical anthropology perspective examines the health policies affecting Aboriginal people, the motivation for this policy becomes questionable (Jacklin and Warry 2004, 215). After the Health Transfer Policy was created, the Assembly of First Nations criticized the policy as a means for the federal government to relinquish its responsibility for health, and as a strategy to cut costs associated with Aboriginal health care. This view is also supported by the Union of Ontario Indians (Jacklin and Warry 2004, 228). Funding would need to increase in relation to community-identified needs arid the demonstrated ability to deliver effective health services. Poor economic conditions and unhealthy communities mean that there is little opportunity to develop self-sustaining resources or a tax base in the foreseeable future (Jacklin and Warry 2004, 229).

Health Canada

Canada's health spending is at 10 percent of GDP, which ranks it as the fourth biggest spender among the countries in the Organization for Economic Cooperation and Development (OECD) (Health Canada 1999).

First Ministers and National Aboriginal Leaders considered the *Blueprint on Aboriginal Health: A 10-Year Transformative Plan* at their meeting in Kelowna, B.C., held November 24–25, 2005. The document responds to the commitment made at the Special Meeting of First Ministers and the Leaders of the Five National Aboriginal Organizations on September 13, 2004. The Blueprint is a roadmap to guide action and investment in closing the gap in health outcomes between First Nations, Inuit, and Métis and Canadians as a whole (Health Canada 2005).

The Government of Canada committed to investing $1.315 billion over the next five years: $870 million to stabilize the First Nation and Inuit Health System, and $445 million to promote transformation and to build capacity (Health Canada 2005). In Ottawa, Ontario on May 31, 2005, the Prime Minister, members of the Cabinet Committee on Aboriginal Affairs, and the leaders of five National Aboriginal Organizations met for a Policy Retreat in a new spirit of cooperation and to address long-term challenges (Health Canada 2005). The leaders of the Assembly of First Nations (AFN), the Inuit Tapiriit Kanatami (ITK), the Métis National Council (MNC), the Congress of Aboriginal Peoples (CAP), and the Native Women's Association of Canada (NWAC) also signed joint accords with the Government of Canada that would ensure their direct involvement in Aboriginal policy development (Health Canada 2005). Agreement was reached on directions for change in health, education/lifelong learning, housing, economic opportunities, negotiations/relationships, and accountability for results (Health Canada 2005).

The Assembly of First Nations agreed that a positive restructuring initiation would include a Network of Health Centres and Lodges that was operated by the First Nations in an integrated service delivery environment. "A funding model that holistically incorporates health and health-related services is compatible with the Aboriginal view of health and well-being. The Medicine Wheel or Circle of Life provides a framework for holistic healing which encompasses physical, mental, emotional, and spiritual domains. Only in the last twenty years has the mainstream health system adopted a similar perspective, one which acknowledges that health and well-being stem from a variety of factors and influences, classified as "broad health determinants." These determinants include social and economic forces, psychological influences, physical and genetic factors, and cultural elements. The importance of health determinants has been validated in numerous studies, which have shown the connection between health status and a number of factors including income, position in society, employment, lifestyle factors, and control over one's personal situation" (Health Canada 2005, 1). For Aboriginal people, holistic healing that interrelates physical, mental, emotional, and spiritual elements will not only restore wellness to individuals, but also renew their capacity to exercise collective responsibility and build caring, inclusive communities (Aboriginal Healing Foundation 1998, note 20). The Royal Commission on Aboriginal Peoples (RCAP), in its final report, identified several areas where Aboriginal health and healing concepts are congruent with the health determinants model:

1. True health comes from the connectedness of human systems, not their separate dynamics. The four components of the healing circle reinforce the results of research on health determinants. "Health is the total effect of vitality in and balance between all life support systems."

2. Economic factors are particularly important in determining the level of health of a population.

3. Responsibility for health is both individual and collective. Personal choices on lifestyle (smoking, diet, exercise, etc.) combined with an individual responsibility for well-being is complementary to Aboriginal perspectives on collective responsibility for community well-being, as well as individual self-care.

4. Aboriginal beliefs regarding good health are based on balance and harmony within oneself and within the social and natural environment. This is echoed in research that has proven causal links between stress and ill health (Health Canada 2005, 2).

To date, no restructuring initiatives have been implemented by the federal government, and the status quo continues today. The federal response has been limited to providing some funding in targeted areas, such as early childhood development, diabetes, housing, sewage infrastructure, some aspects of education reform, water management, and social assistance (Assembly of First Nations 2010).

The Royal Commission on Aboriginal Peoples' Implications for Canada's Health System (RCAP)

The RCAP report (1997) states under the key elements of the Commission's human resources strategy that governments, health authorities, and traditional practitioners will cooperate to protect and extend the practices of traditional healing, and to facilitate dialogue between traditional healers and biomedical healers (The Commission's report contains an Appendix on traditional health and healing—Vol. 3, pages 348 to 361) (Institute On Governance 1997).

The Assembly of First Nations (AFN)

The Assembly of First Nations, in their Royal Commission on Aboriginal People, states the implication for the future is toward Canada's Failure to Act. There is no structural change in the relationship between First Nations and the Canadian government, as recommended by RCAP, no new Royal Proclamation, no national framework to guide treaty discussions, and no Aboriginal Nations Recognition and Governance Act, which would recognize Aboriginal governments as one of the three orders of governance in Canada. There is no abolishment of DIAND, no independent administrative tribunal for lands and treaties, no long-term economic development agreements between First Nations or institutions and federal provincial territorial orders of government, no network of healing centres and lodges under First Nations control, and no legislative changes to allow integrated health service delivery across jurisdictions. There is no commitment to train 10,000 Aboriginal professionals in health and social services in ten years. There is inadequate funding growth for health programs, capped at 3 percent for ten years.

All new targeted health programs announced after 1996/97 do not receive **any** annual growth.

New health program funding, such as Maternal Child Health, is often inadequate, and only selected communities can benefit from the funds. A health funding shortfall of close to $2 billion is expected for five years. Individual communities experience an average gap of 9 percent in 2006/2007 and 14 percent in 2007/2008 between what they will receive in health funding and what is actually needed. There is an overall shortfall of approximately $7.914 billion from the standpoint of the Assembly of First Nations on all restructuring initiatives that the Government of Canada has failed to act upon (Assembly of First Nations 2010).

Integrating Traditional Medicine and Healers in Communities within Canada

Other provinces provide a fuller understanding of the use of traditional medicines and healers and traditional ways of healing within Canada. The following are provinces that utilize and work toward the integration of traditional methods of healing and Western medicine:

Nova Scotia—Traditional Mi'kmaq Medicine

Mi'kmaq medicine is used with patients at a First Nations community health centre in Nova Scotia. The results of a study that addressed cross-cultural care to 100 patients (14 were men and 86 women) showed that 66 percent of the respondents used Mi'kmaq medicine, and 92.4 percent of the respondents had not discussed this with their physicians. Of those who used Mi'kmaq medicine, 24.3 percent used it as their first line of treatment for illness, and 31.8 percent believe that Mi'kmaq medicine is better overall than Western medicine. There were 5.9 percent of patients who did not use the Mi'kmaq medicine but believe that the medicine is more effective than Western medicine. The results of the study imply that understanding patient's health care values is important in the delivery of health care to First Nations patients in order to meet the needs of providing effective cross-cultural care. During the European colonization in the late 1800s, the early Indian Acts were associated with legislation that denied access to traditional medicinal plants and banned traditional healing as "witchcraft." The right to practice traditional healing has been revitalized (Cook 2005, 1).

Former Grand Chief of the Assembly of First Nations Ovide Mercredi stated that one of the reasons for the health problems in the First Nations communities is the destruction of Aboriginal culture; instead of resisting the restoration of the Indian culture, the government should become a partner with Indians in the restoration. In the Royal Commission on Aboriginal Peoples' 1996 Report, four cornerstones were advocated, including "the appropriate use of traditional medicine and healing techniques that will assist in improving outcomes" (Cook 2005, 2). The report expressed sentiment toward "the integration of traditional healing practices and spirituality into medical and social services is the missing ingredient needed to make those services work for Aboriginal people" (Cook 2005, 2). The policy statement by the Society of Obstetricians and Gynecologists of Canada's Aboriginal Health Issues Committee stated that "health professionals should respect traditional medicines and work with Aboriginal healers to seek ways to integrate traditional and Western medicine, and health professionals should appreciate holistic definitions of health as defined by Aboriginal peoples" (Cook 2005, 2). A majority of Mi'kmaq patients surveyed at a First Nations community medical centre use or have used Mi'kmaq medicine in addition to Western medicine, and a large number of patients believe that Mi'kmaq medicine is more effective than Western medicine (Cook 2005, 2–3).

Yukon First Nations—Council for Yukon Indians, Whitehorse, Yukon, Canada

Traditional medicine and practices went underground when Europeans arrived and prohibited traditional medical practices, as the traditional ways of aboriginal peoples stood in the way of the non-Natives' progress (Wheatley 1990, 217–220).

A study was to be researched and developed, the objective of which was to develop an integrated traditional and clinical health system in the Yukon. The study would construct a model for integrating traditional medicine into a Yukon Health Care System. The two main issues were 1) the development of a process for identification and recognition of traditional practices and practitioners to be included in an integrated system, and 2) the policy and legislative procedures necessary to implement such a system. The steps taken by the Yukon First Nations included:

- Making contacts with Health and Legal professionals, traditional healers, and individual Elders;

- Defining Yukon Traditional Medicine;

- Designating an Elder with expertise in or knowledge about traditional medicine to participate in a one-day Council of Elders workshop (community representation).

Topics of discussion included:

- A wide range of plants used throughout the Yukon for similar ailments;

- "New" uses of a particular plant;

- Other practices, such as blood-letting, acupuncture, healing springs, use of bear gall, and the sauna and sweat lodge (physical and spiritual cleansing and purification).

Difficulties Identified by Elders included:

- Identifying recognized traditional healers;

- Cultural values prohibiting nomination without prior consent;

- After years of prohibition and disparagement, uncertainty about current interest;

- Practitioners of traditional medicine are known, but it is still "underground."

Trust had to be established so traditional healers will come forward or be approached to come forward before advancement could be made (Wheatley 1990, 217–220). The Elders' concern was that the process would take time and patience. The process would need the involvement and cooperation of the communities to reach a consensus on how to proceed (Wheatley 1990, 217–220).

The problem with payment and protection was difficult to identify, as "payment" is not clearly defined. Elders are concerned that the knowledge not be lost, but at the same time, by recording it, they expose themselves to losing its value. Several questions that were considered include:

- Will people be paid for their information, and if so, who then owns the information that is bought?

- Traditional medicine is largely oral; can it be protected as well as written down?

- Is it patent or payment that is the goal?

- The problem with payment overlaps with that of ethics and is crucial in trying to develop an integrated system.

- Like malpractice suits in mainstream medical treatments, does there need to be some kind of control over traditional treatments and practitioners, and who would exercise the control? Who is accountable and to whom (Wheatley 1990, 217–220)?

- Healers are accountable to the Creator, but are they accountable to the Elders? Ethical issues are raised (Wheatley 1990, 217–220).

A pluralistic approach (different groups) entails a health care system that can work and be recognized as "traditional" and "Western" within a totally integrated system, with Western and traditional practices working in union with one another. The traditional practitioner is a fully recognized participant within a pluralistic health care system. This model is unlikely because of the basic fundamental differences in beliefs and value systems, which make it difficult to implement. The model of parallel systems with mutual respect and referrals from one to the other is a possibility (Wheatley 1990, 217–220).

The next steps for the Yukon First Nations include:

- A proposal to obtain funding to design a suitable model for an integrated Yukon Indian/clinical health care system that is built on the initial steps taken;

- Following the Elders' advice and with their assistance, communities establish their own projects to record the plants and practices used;

- Communities identify people who use traditional practices and who are willing to come forward;

- Elders and traditional people come together to discuss their concerns (Wheatley 1990, 217–220).

Representatives from the traditional system met with the representatives from the Western system to discuss areas of cooperation. Once the "content" was identified, the model for integrating the two health systems was addressed. Meetings were held with the elders at a one-day workshop during the Yukon winter (1989-90). Old people were moved over great distances. The Yukon Territorial Government officials, legal advisors, medical advisors, and the Yukon First Nations representatives instigated the process. The Yukon Territorial Government indicated a willingness to look at ways of including traditional health care practices for patients who wished to use them (Wheatley 1990, 217–220).

British Columbia's First Nations Health Plan

The First Nations Leadership Council plans are to set into action the government's commitments to the Transformative Change Accord to close the health gap between First Nations and other British Columbians. The First Nations health plan is to support the Health and Wellness of First Nations in British Columbia and ensure First Nations will be integral partners in the design and delivery of health initiatives to close health gaps. Grand Chief Edward John of the First Nations Summit said, "First Nations and regional health authorities will work collaboratively to develop and implement programs that will address adult mental health, substance abuse, youth suicide, maternal health, and programs to help manage chronic health conditions that First Nations face, as diabetes and hepatitis" (Steeves and Adair 2006, 1–2).

The First Nations Health Plan that will support the Health and Wellness of First Nations in British Columbia includes:

- An Aboriginal physician appointed by the Provincial Health Officer to advise on Aboriginal health issues;

- A First Nations/Aboriginal-specific ActNow BC program;

- An Aboriginal Mental Health and Addictions Plan to include healing circles, cultural camps, and counseling programs that build community capacity;

- Improved access to primary health care services in Aboriginal health and healing centres;

- Primary health services and patient self-management programs to help manage chronic health conditions such as diabetes and Hepatitis C;

- A new health centre in Lytton to improve acute care and community health services and better meet the needs of First Nations and other area residents (Steeves and Adair 2006, 1–2).

Ontario—Wikwemikong First Nation

Wikwemikong First Nation in Ontario has had many obstacles to integrating traditional and Western medicines within their community. The Canadian government continues to retain control of First Nations health care. Like other First Nations, Wikwemikong has had a rapid increase in population with high levels of disease and disease projections, and high rates of suicide, depression, and other mental health concerns. Since 1862, the Wikwemikong First Nation has lobbied the federal government for self-government. In 1968, the Wikwemikong Chief and Council passed a resolution to control all services, such as education. A new Health Centre erected a traditional healing lodge with no control over their processes due to the Health Transfer Policy. A resolution was passed by the Band for the pursuit of the transfer of health services (Jacklin and Warry 2004, 220). The handbooks omitted self-determination, with self-government being a separate option from the

Health Transfer. The Wikwemikong Reserve Health Transfer goals are for the provision of holistic health care, and the integration of traditional and Western medicines leading to improved community health. The community health plans and the government policy require an evaluation for effectiveness (Jacklin and Warry 2004, 220–221).

The Anthropological Perspectives
on Aboriginal Societies

The following are anthropological references about Native people's ways of living, and how theorists perceive the "'Native point of view." The research was conducted from the mid-1800s to the present time.

Emile Durkheim

Emile Durkheim (1858–1917) references totemism in *The Cosmological System of Totemism and the Idea of Class.* Durkheim distinguishes three classes, which he recognizes as sacred in varying degrees: the totemic emblem, the animal or plant whose appearance this emblem reproduces, and the members of the clan. Durkheim presents an extremely interesting idea with the totemic organization. He says that the universe is divided among the totems, with each totem having a set of elements identified as part of its economic classification. As the same object is not found in two different totems, the systems complement each other. Thus, when all the clans assemble, an observer is presented with a complete model of the Aboriginal universe. If totemism is to be considered a religion comparable to the others, it too should offer us a conception of the universe (McGee and Warms 2008, 80–90). Durkheim's cosmological system helps illustrate the Anishinaabe Nation cultural and traditional connections to the clan system. The clan system consists of spirit and sacredness in the form of animal spirits, and the relations to the universe. The Bear Clan represents the healer, medicine, and protectors of the people, as all clans represent tribal meaning and have significant meaning to their community.

Franz Boas

In *The Methods of Ethnology*, Franz Boas (1858–1942) reflects on the whole problem of cultural history that appears to us as a historical problem. In order to understand history, it is necessary to know not only how things are, but how they have come to be (McGee and Warms 2008, 124). Boas's principle of "cultural relativism" reflects on the idea that each culture is the product of a unique and particular history, and not merely generated by race and environment. He argues that it is only through living with a people and learning their language that one can develop an accurate understanding of a culture that has a perspective relative to its contexts (McGee and Warms 2008, 361). The principles of integrating traditional medicine and healers into Western clinics is found within Boas's theoretical understanding of culture, and the uniqueness of the Anishinaabe people's traditions that are relative to the Anishinaabe emic views of cultural life. In order for traditional and Western practices to integrate, one must learn the Anishinaabe people's way of life.

Bronislaw Malinowski

Bronislaw Malinowski (1884–1942), in *Argonauts of the Western Pacific*, wrote that the final goal of ethnography was "to grasp the native's point of view, his relation to life, to realize his vision of the world" (McGee and Warms 2008, 361). If the Western and traditional mind-sets came together to discuss the issues, concerns, and possibilities of an integrated health care system for First Nations peoples, by grasping the native's point of view in relation to a healthy lifestyle, the outcomes and benefits could have a profound effect on the wellness of aboriginal peoples today.

Claude Levi-Strauss

Claude Levi-Strauss's (1908–2009) structuralism is a product of the mind; since all human brains are biologically similar; he reasoned that there must be deep-seated similarities among cultures. Levi-Strauss set out to discover the fundamental structure of human cognition and underlying patterns of human thought that produce the great variety of current and historical cultures. Levi-Strauss spent his career conducting cross-cultural studies of kinship, myths, and religion. Strauss's analysis of myth and interest in mythology lies in his belief that studying the mythologies of primitive peoples allows him to examine the unconscious universal patterning of human thought in its least contaminated form. Levi-Strauss's view is that the mythology of primitive peoples is closer to these universal principles than are Western beliefs, because the training received in Western society buries the logical structure under layers of "cultural interference" created by our social environment (McGee and Warms 2008, 324–325). Levi-Strauss's view is that aspects of cultural interference are primarily a cross-cultural pattern of misunderstandings between traditional and Western societies that evolved over time, into our makeshift societies of today. Western and traditional integration can only exist if, as Levi-Strauss in his works hopes, "by breaking down cultures into their elemental parts, [one] could get beyond the 'noise' and return to the original message." The noise is the transmitting of culture that gets jumbled and is the result of the particular history and technological adaptation of each culture. The processes have combined, altered, transfigured, and modified the original bits of information. When we consider the implications of colonialism, assimilation processes, and residential school systems from a diachronic (through time) perspective, there are patterns of cultural interference from a synchronic (same time frame) perspective today. First Nations today seek to embrace their cultures and traditions without interference from the mainstream society, so that cultural patterns of growth can be formed by those that carry the transmitted sacred messages to heal their people.

Marcel Mauss

Marcel Mauss (1872–1950), in his book *Excerpts from the Gift*, discusses the reciprocity that exists in First Nations communities' cultural systems. The obligation to give and the obligation to receive is the essence of the potlatch of the Northwest peoples of Canada. The spirit of the gift is a widespread, if not universal, institution. If we consider Mauss's reflection on societies that stabilize through their contracts to give, receive, and repay, in order to trade, man must first lay down his spear. When that is done, he can succeed in exchanging goods with persons not only between clan and clan, but between tribe and tribe, nation and nation, and above all, between individuals. It is only then that people can create, can satisfy their interests mutually, and can define them without recourse to arms. It is in this way that the clan, the tribe, and the nation have learned how to oppose one another without slaughter and to give without sacrificing themselves to others. That is one of the secrets of their wisdom and solidarity (McGee and Warms 2008, 94–95). According to *Excerpts of the Gift*, the gift is symbolic to First Nations peoples of how they give and receive to one another in the exchange of tobacco—*simaa* (sacred medicine). Within the Anishinaabe culture and traditions, when a person seeks spiritual guidance and healing from traditional healers, tobacco is passed along with a gift to the healer. When First Nations peoples work with wisdom and solidarity to benefit their communities' needs, there is help for future generations. First Nations' pleas to Western societies often are opposed when

First Nations request assistance to have traditional medicine and healers attend community members' health needs on a regular basis that would help to heal the people. Reciprocity is necessary for individuals to learn without having to sacrifice themselves to benefit others. This can be applied to integrating traditional and Western practices to ensure First Nations peoples will be able to use their traditional healers and traditional medicinal practices.

Beatrice Medicine

Beatrice Medicine (1923–2005), a Lakota Sioux woman from South Dakota, wrote *Learning to Be an Anthropologist and Remaining Native*, which include the essay "My Elders Tell Me." The essay reflects on Elders being the repositories and transmitters of cultural and philosophical knowledge. On the Morley Reserve, Indian Ecumenical Conferences were held from 1970 to 1984, and during this time, John Snow observed, "During these conferences, many Indian elders, medicine men, and women taught us our basic beliefs and teachings, encouraging us to continue with our faith in the Great Spirit, the Creator." The basic beliefs and teachings have continued through North America within the matrices of various Native Indian households, traditions, language, and participation in rituals and ceremonies that are grounded in the culture of a specific tribal or band group. The continuity of these cultural manifestations accounts for the viability and vibrancy of Indian cultures embedded in their Elders (Beatrice 2001, 73). When culture and traditions are taught by traditional Anishinaabe elders, the truth and vitality of a culture comes alive in the oral idiom of ancestral teachings. In order to pass on the Anishinaabe culture and traditions, knowledgeable elders and medicine people must take a stand in their communities and teach the community members about the need to utilize the doctoring methods of medicine people and traditional medicines to heal their mind, body, and spirit. Beatrice Medicine reflects on this very metaphor of traditional teachings for the continuity of culture and traditions for many generations to come. The findings from this research reflect the need to educate through traditional workshops, taught by customary elders and medicine people, to be held in the communities to teach community members about traditional medicine, traditional medicine people, and traditional life.

Michel Foucault

Michel Foucault's theories and writing on the "body politic" and the writings of other contemporary and postmodern thinkers advocate liberating "health" from the restrictions of the biomedical model, creating frames of reference beyond disease and illness (Parlee and O'Neil 2007, 112–113).

The body politic that Foucault describes essentially moves away from the biomedical model of health into a Medicine Wheel model of health that traditional healers engage in when working with illness in the body. Traditional ways of treating illness work with the emotional (social), physical, mental, and spiritual aspects of the human body.

Brenda Parlee, John O'Neil

"The Dene Way of Life: Perspectives on Health from Canada's North," by Brenda Parlee, John O'Neil, and The Lutsel K'e Dene First Nation, suggests that there is little consideration given to how health is conceptualized in Aboriginal communities. The health of Canada's Aboriginal population has been a focus of study and policy development for decades. The inequality of the level of effort and resources between the health of Inuit, Métis, and First Nations peoples and other Canadians remains significant. "Irrespective of the health indicator used, Canadian Aboriginal peoples tend to bear a disproportionate burden of ill health. The rising incidence of disease such as diabetes raises questions about the efficacy of the current health paradigm." What is required is to "rethink the applicability of different models of intervention from the perspective of local community values and aspirations." Improving the applicability of health care requires rethinking not only medical practice, but also the meaning of "health." Epidemiological knowledge constructs an understanding of Aboriginal society that reinforces unequal power relationships, an image of sick and disorganized communities that can be used to justify patterns of paternalism and dependency (Parlee et al. 2007, 112–114). Looking at communities in terms of their needs and problems serves only to increase individual dependence on experts and professionals, robbing them of the ability to care for themselves and each other. Indigenous peoples refer to health and wellness as a balance between the emotional, mental, spiritual, and physical dimensions of the person in connection to his or her family and community. Other scientists suggest meanings that emphasize social relationships and spirituality as well as the land. A Whapmagoostui Cree elder said, "If the land is not healthy, how can we be?" (Parlee and O'Neil 2007, 112–114). If we are to rethink cultural and traditional ways of healing within First Nations communities, there will be a need to implement and integrate a traditional Native health care system so that healers can heal people through traditional healing practices. Rethinking cultural and traditional ways of healing will assist Native communities who are faced with high levels of health issues.

Theorists and theory provide an anthropological understanding from years of research from the 1800s to present. Today, we can draw on the anthropological work of early and present scientists to help us to better understand indigenous societies historically—and today. Through the theoretical contexts provided by anthropologists, the options to pursue research projects such as "Integrating Traditional Medicine and Healers into Western Clinics" can be much more explanatory and provide associations to evidence-based studies that are supportive and significant to understanding concepts within ethnographic studies.

THE RESEARCH COMPONENT

Anthropological fieldwork on the integration of traditional medicine and healers into Western medical clinics was conducted from May 2010 to December 2010. The Institutional Review Board of the University of North Texas reviewed and approved this project. The research project was conducted for the North Shore Tribal Council Health Centre, with approvals from the Chief and Councils of the autonomous First Nations of Garden River, Batchewana (Rankin), and the Sault Ste. Marie Indian Friendship Centre Executive Director.

Research Population

The prime locations for the purposes of the research project were Sault Ste. Marie, Batchewana, and Garden River.

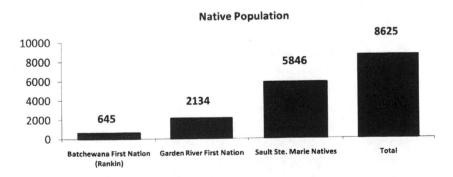

Native Population

Statistics Canada 2010

City of Sault Ste. Marie (Total 74,948, 2006)

Data Collection

Data for this project was collected from 1) the Director of the N'Mninoeyaa Aboriginal Health Access Centre; 2) health professional service providers; 3) clients of the centre; 4) traditional healers; 5) clients of traditional healers; and 6) a sweat lodge ceremony.

Key Participant Interview: I conducted a key participant interview with the director of the N'Mninoeyaa Aboriginal Health Access Centre in order to obtain detailed information on the health services offered. Topics included major health problems, how these health problems can be overcome, and how the health centre can enhance access to traditional healing.

Surveys: I conducted survey research with two different samples—the health professional service providers at the centre and the clients of the centre.

Health Professional Service Providers: Service providers (n=13) were asked questions regarding the major health problems of the communities they serve, the extent to which traditional healing is used in these communities, their knowledge of how well traditional healing contributes to positive health outcomes, and barriers to integrating traditional healing with biomedicine. The survey was distributed at the Centre through the director.

Clients of the Centre: Clients of the centre were surveyed in order to gain a better understanding of the client use of traditional methods of healing both within their communities and outside of their communities (Batchewana First Nations n=4, Garden River First Nation n=10, and the Sault Ste. Marie Natives n=8, for a total of 22 participants). Topics of investigation included major health problems, the extent to which they use traditional healing and biomedicine, their perception of how well traditional healing is treating their bodies, and their ideas about how traditional healing can be better incorporated in the biomedical centre. These surveys were distributed by me and through the service providers as they visit their clients in the three communities.

Semi-structured Interviews: I conducted semi-structured interviews with two different samples—traditional healers and clients of traditional healers.

Traditional Healers: Semi-structured interviews were conducted with traditional healers (n=6) from Garden River First Nation, Serpent River First Nation, and the Sault Tribe of Chippewas.

The topics ranged from whether they consider themselves to be medicine people, personal differences of opinion, common health problems and remedies, number of people they doctor, how they doctor, and conducting ceremonies. How do healers perceive the integration process and its value for the community people? What is the personal vision that healers have for individuals, government, and First Nations participation in traditional methods of healing?

Clients of Traditional Healers: Semi-structured interviews were conducted with clients of healers from Batchewana (Rankin) n=2, Garden River First Nation n=2; Sault Ste. Marie Natives n=2. They were selected by convenience sampling through recommendations from health centres and healers' clients. The topics included the doctoring recommendations by the healers, their perceptions of health improvement, how traditional healing may affect their biomedical doctor visits, how often they seek healers for care, if they travel to be doctored by a healer, and whether it is worthwhile and accommodating for healers to be as available as biomedical doctors are available.

Observations: Participation observations were conducted at a sweat lodge at the Garden River First Nation. The purpose of the participant observations was to understand how ceremonies are essential to the process of healing people. In understanding the ceremonial processes, the research project will present information conducive to ceremonial rituals, protocols, and spiritual healing that revolves around the use of sacred medicines, sacred pipes, spiritual interactions, and specific directions that are given to individuals. Participant observations at ceremonial healing practices provide an understanding of how individuals are healed by traditional healers compared to Western methods of healing.

Results
Traditional Medicine and Healers among the Anishinaabe

This section provides an overview of the healing techniques and availability of Anishinaabe healers. The Anishinaabe way of life reflects an oral history, and storytelling is a means of bringing about the true concept of the Anishinaabe culture and tradition. Much of this report is through storytelling.

Healers utilize a variety of ceremonies to heal the sick. The healers conduct ceremonies from sweat lodges to shaking tents, to pipe ceremonies, to hands on healing, to cedar bath ceremonies, to fasting and feasting, to harvesting and making medicine, and to drumming, singing, and dancing to our heartbeat, the heartbeat of Mother Earth. Traditional healing, traditional medicine, and ceremonies are known to cure illnesses that address the emotional, physical, mental, and spiritual well-being of people.

The following storytelling illustrates the Native healers' views:

The healers conduct spiritual ceremonies; they take the plant's spirit so that the spirit can heal. "We can take the plant, but the medicine plants are the difference in that the medicines are out there growing from the Great Spirit, but I cannot separate medicine from spirit," says the "the one who doctors" (Francis), *naan dawi ji ge – nini*[17] (Healer Interviews 2010).

---

17   Ojibwe word for "the one who doctors."

Leonard, who conducts sweat lodges[18] and circles, along with fire keeping, talked about following spirit when you are performing the ceremonies. He said, "You might have a 120 people in the room, but yet you might pick someone out and smudge[19] them, and they come up and tell you after that they needed that without the people even realizing it" (Healer Interviews 2010).

Mabel spoke about cedar bath ceremonies and how they heal people. For example, she said, "A person can go to a cedar bath and all of sudden they bring up mucus. That is a healing that is happening; it can happen in a sweat and can happen with hands-on healing. They can move that out of you. People have the ability to move that mucus out" (Healer Interviews 2010).

Mabel gave an example of healing that occurred with her son. She said, "My son got a bacterial infection in his leg and was crying about his pain. I took him to emergency and they said there was nothing wrong. My son asked me to take the pain away. I took him back home. I did not know what to do, so I prayed. A medicine came to me, and all of a sudden I got some plantain. I got the medicine, put it on his leg, and returned to the doctor. The plantain drew it up to the surface; before that they could not see anything. If I knew what I know now, I could have put that medicine on there, drawn it up, and taken it right out. At the time I did not have that base knowledge of the medicine to know to cut the skin surface so it would come through ... if I had not done that, it may have gone into his bone" (Healer Interview 2010).

Bill spoke about his father who said, "When you pick the medicine, get up with the sun. When the medicine rests, it goes to sleep with the sun that goes down. The highest level of energy that the medicine can have is at high noon because that is when the sun is at its highest. So go by that day. I don't think he picked medicine when it was overcast or cloudy" (Healer Interview 2010).

Bill's advice on healing people is that "one thing I've learnt is you can't change a person's life. All you can do is show them a good life, and let them change. I don't know how a person can be liable when they have chosen to change." Bill is referring to liability when working with clients who choose traditional healing (Healer Interview 2010).

Mabel believes "a true healer is not somebody that has read something and works with it from that, but someone who has actually claimed that relationship with that plant, and I can give you an example. Faith knows a lot about the plants, but she also has that relationship with those plants. I

18   Sweat lodge, traditional sacred healing ceremony, cleansing and healing from the grandfathers and grandmothers (stones); spiritual healing ceremony that is headed by a knowledgeable conductor.
19   Purification, cleansing with sacred medicine such as sage.

think that the difference is between someone who is educated in a sense about plants can do certain things with plants and traditional medicine people. If you want to give it a name, they have a relationship with those plants, and a spiritual connection with those plants. If I was going to give you medicine for a certain illness, there are so many different plants that are for that illness. When the simaa tobacco is passed to the healer, then the healer will work with that tobacco, and his spirit, and your spirit. You might take a different medicine than someone else. They might have their main medicine, but they might add certain things for you personally, as a patient. If we are going to use a traditional way of thinking, that individual passed tobacco and has asked something of the healer so that is the contract they made with one another. A patient of a medicine person or traditional doctor has to pass tobacco, and that is the contract they have made with one another. Now if you think that the healer has to do the work, he does not have too. He has to get the answer and provide it to you. Go and see so and so, they will help you with that. That is how I would look at the traditional contract" (Healer Interview 2010).

Methods that are used by First Nations peoples include the Medicine Wheel[20]. Mabel said, "I think the Medicine Wheel is important with all issues you are dealing with, because we as aboriginal people do not deal with one piece of the pie. We deal with the whole pie. For example, if someone came with a headache, there could be physical, mental, spiritual, or emotional reasons for it happening to them. If they only focus on the physical part of that headache, then they are not seeing the whole picture. I think it is important to use that whole picture when you are working with healing an individual" (Healer Interviews 2010).

Mabel described the Anishinaabe relationship with the medicines. She said, "Medicines in their natural form are not commercialized, or tampered with, or made with synthetic things to give them higher potency, as is the Western practice. The traditional medicine people have a spiritual relationship with the natural plants. When we gather a plant, we always put our tobacco down, but we actually have a relationship with that plant asking that plant what we need it for and that kind of spiritual relationship." She recommended not changing that relationship. "The only thing I would do in that process would be to incorporate pin cherry medicine in a bag that is going directly into the blood, to do that healing work, say for someone who cannot swallow the medicine." Mabel said that the integration would improve the health of people (Healer Interviews 2010).

Lillie has a connection to the Creator. Lillie reflected on a client who amazed her at one point by what she does for healing. Part of her spirit had

---

20   The Anishinaabe or Ojibwa nation has a teaching that the Medicine Wheel is
     the circle of life (Beaver, 2009).

left when she started experiencing abuse, and that was what the client was looking for. She said, "It was almost like they were searching and searching all over the place, and they didn't know what the heck they were searching for. We started to incorporate taking them on a journey, bringing the Creator into their journey for them, to see in their third eye. They see the little spirit, and I ask them who the little spirit is. They would say, 'That is me.' Getting that little spirit back and honoring that before all that time had started is what I find has really really worked" (Healer Interviews 2010).

Lillie works with the spirit of the person. When she does the cedar bath ceremonies on people, she will find a ball in the chest, and the person complains about pain. Their stomach is sore, and they have aches and pains in the chest area. She calls it "shit," and says we carry a lot of it. A lot of times we get down into there, and if we do that in a spiritual sense, we can get into do the physical healing. It gives the person a more open awareness to heal, and they are not all closed off. Lillie says, "If you look at Western compared to traditional, traditional looks at all of them together—your mental, your emotional, and your physical, as well as your spiritual. Western looks at the pain and the physical. Western is not looking at it as a whole, and access to traditional possibilities to help individuals within our community will be more successful, by looking at all four, as opposed to looking at symptoms that go to the root of some problems, as they are all interconnected" (Healer Interviews 2010).

Lillie says that "working with spirits is not something that is out there (physical realm), nor is it something you can see (spiritual realm). The Creator gives us that third eye in the middle of our forehead. You can see light and you may be sitting on a rock. I will ask them to get the light to come toward them, and ask them what they see. They say there is a little person there. The Creator gives us these pictures for us to understand. These people say, 'Wow, I actually saw that'" (Healer Interview 2010).

Mabel said, "Medicine people have different ways of doing their healing. The sweat lodge [see below] is used for some healers and medicine is passed. Other healers work with the plants and tree medicines, having a relationship to the medicine in that way. They all use spirit to guide them to make the medicine. There are not different modalities of doing it; there are different ceremonies and conductors who will perform various ceremonies such as the shaking tent[21]. The shaking tents may not do medicine, but they give guidance. There is a relationship through spirit and the ancestors. The person may receive a message through there that they need to take this type of medicine" (Healer Interviews 2010).

---

21   Shaking tent is a spiritual ceremony used by Native people who connect with spirits to obtain answers, and for healing purposes.

Francis reflected on his journey as a healer. He said, "According to a legend that my elders gave me when I was a young man, there is what they call the traveling man. It is pretty much what I have been doing. It is like the language in the way they explained it. I would travel many many trails, and then I would go on one that I had not been on before, and that is where I would stay. I don't know when that legend is going to end. I was told this legend when I was twenty years old." Francis's guidance came from his elders who crossed his path. This is how many Native people find their way and purpose in life that the Creator has provided to individuals. The Anishinaabe word for where a person is going in life is *e-kinomaagozit* (Healer Interviews 2010).

The ceremonies that were mentioned were sweat lodges, full moon, circles, sacred fires, feasting ancestors, cedar baths, seven grandfathers, detoxification teaching/learning sweat lodges, sacred pipe ceremonies, and shaking tent ceremonies (Healer Interviews 2010).

Availability of Healers

There are sporadic times that healers heal; it is much different from the Western mind-set of structured timetables and scheduling appointments. Healing and ceremonies are not timed, but occur when the time is right to conduct and heal people.

The healers' hours varied, depending on the type of healing or what ceremonies they conducted. Bill said he works with eighty to ninety clients a month, about three ceremonies a week. The number of people at each ceremony varies. Lillie works with at least six people and up to twenty-one persons a day. Leonard does about three sweats a month. He said, "They do grieving ceremonies, smudging and drumming ceremonies, teachings for some, and ceremonies for some, over a hundred in one month." Mabel does about ten ceremonies in a month. Tom does not record the number of people he heals, and he cannot keep up with the demand. He has received calls from as faraway places as Egypt and the Virgin Islands. He has made medicine for many people from many different places. As for Francis, he does about twenty-five a day, and thirty-five when he is on the road. The average is 350 people a month at about 450 ceremonies in a month (Healer Interviews 2010).

Leonard mentioned that "Native doctoring does not have a time on it. They can be there all day and all night" (Healer Interviews 2010).

Places traditional healers perform their healing

There are many places that healers heal and doctor people, but preferences are sacred spiritual grounds, in sweat lodges, and in traditional healing lodges where a sacred fire burns. For some, as long as the healing is performed in a positive way, it can be done anywhere. The following are quotes from healers who mention their preferences:

The communities determine where to best serve their members. "Healing can take place at the Powwow grounds, and just about anywhere that works best for the community members," said the Health Director. The healers had similar answers about where they would prefer to perform their healing. The most prominent healing places are the healing lodges, where there is a sacred fire burning in a calming environment, and where you are out in nature seeing animals around you. The outdoors is found to be a stronger place, especially around spiritual grounds. Francis said, "I prefer spiritual grounds; if I had my ideal place I would be at the Midewewin spiritual grounds, or at an outside spiritual setting in each community. I like to do the healing in the woods in the bush around nature" (Healer Interviews 2010).

Others agreed with Lillie, who commented, "I don't think it really matters where it happens as long as it happens in a positive way." Some healers perform healing at their own homes, such as Bill, who said, "I will do some out of the house, and I will also go out of the community, and work with different communities, too. I do healing in the sweat lodge, or I have a gazebo at home with a fire pit in the middle. I will do healing at palliative care, or intensive care, and sometimes at funeral homes" (Healer Interviews 2010).

Nontraditional places included the Native health centres, and other health clinics, private homes, seniors' homes, and First Nations and American clinics. A healer can be drawn to heal someone who is sick in the backseat of a car on the highway, meeting people from afar (Healer Interviews 2010). Mabel said, "The clinic should be embracing the healing lodge. They should be embracing traditional and contemporary medicine, where they start to work together" (Healer Interviews 2010).

Choice of Payments by Healers

There is a challenge of payment for healing by healers when they are offered sacred tobacco. Some people are not educated about providing a gift to the healer, which can help healers with their expenses to harvest, make, and provide medicine for sick people. Healers are paid in many different ways, and the subject of discussion is that they are valuable and knowledgeable healers who doctor people. Following are explanations about payments or gifts made to healers.

The healers agree that traditional healers should be paid the same as Western doctors. At present, one healer is paid by the Ontario Health Insurance Plan (OHIP), some are paid through health centres, an American clinic, other funding, and some are paid for their time, gas, meals, and a place to stay. The amounts range from a gift to gas, to $250 dollars a day, $2,000 a month, and $2,000 a day, while one may not receive an honorarium, tobacco, or a gift, and incur costs associated with healing people (Healer Interviews 2010).

Traditionally, tobacco is offered as a way of communicating to the healer for spiritual guidance from spirit guides. Costs are incurred by healers for going out and picking the medicines, making the medicines, and shipping the medicines in some cases. One healer (Tom) assists more non-Native people than Native people. He said, "It cost me $130 to ship the medicine to Detroit. I started dealing with Purolator, and it cost me no more than $30 bucks. There was a time when I would work till three o'clock in the morning. I was making about 30, 40, 60 gallons a week, and I was shipping it all over. There was this one guy, he said, 'Send me some more medicine.' I said, 'You are going to have to pay.' He said no, he did not want to pay. He was a millionaire." This is abuse to the medicine person. Mabel said, "The process is to make sure you pass the tobacco, but a healer cannot live on tobacco. There is a cost to the healers to go into the bush and get the medicine. There is also a cost to process the medicine." Mabel says that patients should give what they can give, but never put themselves in jeopardy. "A lot of people are teaching others to just pass tobacco. That is abuse if they do not give something for what they receive." She says, "I think that is the wrong teaching as that is teaching abuse. They need to teach people that they need to give something, think about what they might need and pray about it. In the past, they would have given a horse or a blanket, corn, or potatoes, or whatever that healer could use" (Healer Interviews 2010).

Francis said, "If I took money for ceremony and prayed for you, if I asked for money, it would not work. Money is there instead of healing ... we just ask for tobacco. We do not get paid. It isn't for us, it's for the spirits. But you know in the traditional way you have a healer, a special person who can heal, and can do ceremony, and can help you get well from sickness. It is our Anishinaabe responsibility to take that. It is the way it has been told to me, not that I am getting paid for doing things. This community is looking after me, so I don't have to go out to work at the railway, or work at the electrical company and work for forty hours a work, and then do my work in the evenings. This community is looking after me that way. There are a lot of communities even today, they don't have a healer. There is none in their communities. That is the dilemma now. I could work 10 hours a day every day of the week including weekends right now, if I wanted to, and go to every community, and keep going, and not stop. It would probably kill me in a couple of years" (Healer Interviews 2010).

Francis reflected on being paid, and thinks that money will stop the ceremonies. He said, "If I said to you, I can heal you if you give me $200, that is probably not going to work anyway, but I have $200. Some people say you are getting paid to be there. I am not being paid to do my ceremonies; I am paid to be away from my family, my community, my home, to be with your people. Lots of times, I lose out on a life. This weekend, yesterday, it was my nephew's graduation. I missed it because I was out here working with people. I've missed my nieces' and my own granddaughter's graduation." Francis says the American non-Native clinics should be honored to be integrated, and that Anishinaabe people are in their clinic. He said, "I think they should pay them exactly what they pay their non-Native doctors, because our healers are special" (Healer Interviews 2010).

There are other ways healers are paid for their healing practices. A sweat lodge conductor, Leonard, said he is not paid but sometimes people give him a gift afterward. Lillie's story is different. Lillie said, "I am paid for my time, my gas, my meals, and my place to stay." Healers are paid in some way, whether it is in the form of a gift (reciprocity), or by their expenses being paid for by the organization, or by the client who seeks healing (Healers Interviews 2010).

Mabel said that her father-in-law was a medicine person but would never say he was a medicine man. He would say, "It flows from the Creator, and I am a helper to the Creator." Mabel was told by her father-in-law that we could never pay for what our health is worth; however, to keep the circle going, we need to give to receive, and be grateful. She said, "The system has been abused by some traditional healers who ask for big amounts of money for healing work. It is questionable if a healer is asking $1500 to do healing. If they are going to pay a doctor to come into a clinic, why not pay a medicine person to be in that clinic? They will pay for someone to go see a traditional healer, but they do not want to pay for the healer" (Healer Interviews 2010). Mabel goes on to say, "We tend to pay our people like slave labor and pay the doctor through the roof. Some healers are worth what you are giving, and the same with the doctors. Some doctors are good, and some are not good. I would not undercut them and try to get them for the least we can" (Healer Interviews 2010).

Bill does not refuse honoraria for doing healing work, and says, "It is an embarrassment, a slap in the face, if you turn it down. Put a price on my life; I cannot put a price on it. If people have tobacco, and all they have is tobacco, then that is the reward you get, and if you are given $20 for gas, than you take that." Bill continued, "Healers should go on the pay scales just like the Western [doctors]. Our elders carry a lot of knowledge; a lot of things pass down from generation to generation. The pay scale is just as good as the guy with the diploma" (Healer Interviews 2010).

Francis shared a story about a non-Native doctor being paid by the day. A white diabetes specialist came in and was paid $5000 a day. Francis said, "The relative scale should be that of a specialist, what they pay a specialist. It is our Native communities' responsibility to our healers to look after them financially, because they give up a huge amount for people's wellness. People see a healer there and say they are going to go there because they are sick. They don't consider the healer's well-being. He was really sick, and couldn't get out of bed. There were people coming, and they were demanding to be doctored, our Anishinaabe people" (Healer Interviews 2010).

The Sweat Lodge Ceremony

A participant observation was done on the sweat lodge ceremony to provide the spiritual healing that is portrayed when individuals seek to be cleansed, prayed for, and healed and receive guidance when attending a spiritual ceremony. The following describes the ceremonial practice of healing.

The participant observation of the sweat lodge ceremony was held at the Garden River healing lodge spiritual grounds. The conductor was Leonard, and the ceremony was called by Bill from the Indian Friendship Centre for individuals who asked for healing. The sweat lodge has a capacity to fit thirty to thirty-five people in a double roll. It is a bear lodge, and under the altar is a buried bear skull. The conductor shared a story about a full-grown bear walking into the lodge when ceremony was not being held; this is considered a good sign from nature, from the bear spirit. The sweat lodge preparation commences in the early morning when the sacred fire is ignited by a sacred flint. The sweat lodge has twenty-eight grandfathers (large stones) that are spirits that are brought into the sweat lodge, and placed in a round hole in the ground that is symbolic of a mother's womb, our mother earth, and the womb of all women who carry life (Participant Observation July 2010).

The ceremonial process consists of participants who seek healing. The participants at this sweat lodge consisted of one male conductor, three men, two women, and two children that were five and two years old. In the first round, the conductor's helper brings in seven hot stones on a pitch fork to place them in the open hole in the middle of the sweat lodge. In the second round, there are seven stones, and in the last round there are fourteen. The numbers of stones have meaning: seven is for cleansing, fourteen is for healing, twenty-one is for hunting, and twenty-eight is for truth (drug and alcohol healing). The conductor will ask the people waiting to go in if anyone is asking for their spirit name. A tobacco offering is given to the conductor for this request. The conductor smudges outside and inside the lodge to purify and cleanse the lodge, before anyone enters the sacred ceremony. In a mixed lodge of men and women, individuals prepare to dress for the ceremony. Men dress in shorts and women dress in skirts, or nightgowns. Women need to fully cover their bodies. Each person brings a towel into the sweat lodge for purposes of tears, sickness, and sweat. The conductor's helpers will smudge everyone entering once they walk around the outside of the lodge. Each person will take tobacco and walk around the sacred fire, praying for their needs, personally and for others, and putting tobacco into the sacred fire that holds the spirit stones (grandfathers—whole stones, and grandmothers—split stones). The sacred fire is surrounded by a crescent moon that faces the east door of the lodge and is aligned with the altar that is located just in front of the eastern door. A sacred path of cedar is usually laid down in the lodge, around the opening that is the womb, and a cedar path goes out to the fire and around the fire. This is symbolic of an umbilical cord. This ritual is performed by women only. Sacred items such as drums, rattles, eagle feathers, cloth ties, and sacred pipes are part of the ceremony. The drum is the heartbeat of Mother Earth, and the sacred pipe connects us to the Creator. Outside the lodge is an altar made from the earth in a small mound. This is where the sacred items are placed until it is time to ask that they be brought in and passed around the circle to those who carry sacred objects (Participant Observation July 2010).

The sacred fire is sheathed by the crescent moon that has a large stone on top of the earth mound; this is symbolic of a water boy spirit that experienced the teachings of the sweat lodge ceremony through a vision—a vision that came to be. Upon entering the lodge, if you have your spirit name and clan, you enter by acknowledging yourself so the spirits will know you. A cedar water pail is brought in, along with a brush made of cedar to clean the stones, and to wet the grandfathers and grandmothers that are brought into the lodge to help us. A Y-shaped branch is used to move and place the stones in the hole in the ground fittingly. Steam comes from the stones when the cedar water is added; this is considered medicine, and other medicines can be shared in the circle, or put on the stones for healing, such as small pieces of cedar (Participant Observation July 2010).

There are three rounds in this ceremony. In the first round, traditional songs are sung to welcome the spirits. In the second round, there is sharing and praying is always being conducted in the lodge by the participants. This is a time of releasing and receiving healing, a time when we give up to the Creator what we do not need to carry in our lives. There was loud grunting and yelling that occurred and that sounded like a moose call, when the sweat first commenced. In the sweat lodge, there are four directions, and in each direction spirits come to the ceremony to be with us. The participants are called out when it is time to open the eastern door. The sacred pipe is brought in to share in the circle, along with traditional food such as berries, fish, and corn. Candy is brought in for the little people (*pahiinsag*[22]) spirits. Once the sweat lodge ceremony is over, the water bucket is passed out, and the conductor tells everyone to put tobacco in the fire. All participants give thanks to the conductor and the helper—and to Bill for calling the ceremony for those who needed healing. Everyone coming out is spiritually cleansed, red, sweaty, and hot from being in the lodge. Tobacco is put in the fire, and then everyone sits around outside, cooling off and drinking water. The rugs that were put down in the lodge are taken out to hang and dry on ropes from tree to tree. The sacred fire continues to burn, and then there is gratitude for the healing. See Appendix C for a depiction of a sweat lodge (Participant Observation July 2010).

N'Mninoeyaa Aboriginal Health Access Centre

This description of the Western health centre comes almost entirely from an interview conducted with the Health Director of the centre. Her story helps us to understand the health centre's health care system, and how the system works within the First Nations across the North Shore Tribal Council catchment area. The Health Director describes the health centre as an administrative office that provides a primary health care service delivery model. Health care workers go on site and provide health care to their members in their communities (Personal Interview May 20, 2010).

The N'Mninoeyaa Aboriginal Health Access Centre provides services and works in conjunction with the partner First Nations working with the Health Directors in disease prevention activities through a holistic approach to health from an individual perspective. Nurse practitioners, physicians, and registered dieticians are supplied, along with occupational physiotherapist services and a program that provides seniors with a long-term care agent at home. Nurse case managers help seniors who are being discharged from the hospitals and work with the discharge planners and CTRC to foster safe environments for clients returning home.

The service delivery model includes a lot of travel for the health professionals, which causes loss of clinic time. There is a need for more mental health services because of the limited numbers of services presently available. There is also a need to continuously look for funding and to find more services by working in partnership with the First Nations to link to external services, in order to avoid trying to invent services. This will allow clients to be better served (Personal Interview May 20, 2010).

Poverty is a factor that contributes to health problems and health issues,

22   Pahiinsag is the Ojibwe word for little people or elves.

107

and is a leading problem associated with poor diet. There needs to be sufficient money in a household to spend on good food. Dieticians need to understand and be creative when working with large families, when they counsel and promote diets in the communities. Motivational interviews are conducted that last a half hour in order to find out the real issues that affect the client's health. There is an allotted time per client so that the health professional may take the time to listen to the client's stories. The poverty issues that clients face are very prevalent. The Health Director says change is hard to measure, and clients may still be facing the problems but have a much better way in which to cope with their problems (Personal Interview May 20, 2010).

First Nations peoples in Canada suffer from a poorer quality of life, measured by mortality and morbidity, as compared to their non-Aboriginal counterparts. The average life expectancy of Registered Indians is approximately six years less than the overall Canadian population (Wilson, Rosenberg 2002, 2017). Overcrowded housing not only leads to rapid degeneration of the housing unit, but as is suggested by T. Kue Young et al., rates of "respiratory, skin, and eye infections and tuberculosis, meningitis, and measles have been found to be higher in crowded households; at least this is the case in the Treaty 3 housing crisis (Young et al. in Robson 2008, 80). This housing crisis is a health factor that affects the lives of First Nations peoples across Canada.

Major Health Problems

These are the major health problems of the region according to the health director, healers, health professionals, and clients: diabetes, foot ulcers (diabetic feet), drug addictions and abuse of prescription drugs such as Oxycontin, alcoholism, substance abuse, mental health issues, post-traumatic stress disorder, past trauma, stress, hypertension, anxiety, dementia, depression, schizophrenia, residential school syndrome passed down, sexual abuse, abuse, fetal alcohol syndrome (FAS), ADHD, autism, cancer of the bones, breasts, heart, lungs, liver, and brain, and leukemia, dyslipidemia[23], COPD[24], heart and disease, CVA[25], and other cardiovascular diseases, kidney disease, renal

---

23   Dyslipidemia is a disorder of lipoprotein metabolism, including lipoprotein overproduction or deficiency. Dyslipidemias may be manifested by elevation of the total cholesterol, the "bad" low-density lipoprotein (LDL) cholesterol and the triglyceride concentrations, and a decrease in the "good" high-density lipoprotein (HDL) cholesterol concentration in the blood. Dyslipidemia comes under consideration in many situations, including diabetes, a common cause of lipidemia (Medterms 2010).

24   COPD, or Chronic Obstructive Pulmonary Disease, a disease that affects smokers in large numbers (Medterms 2010).

25   A cerebrovascular accident causes the sudden death of some brain cells due

failure, kidney stones, bladder infections, high blood pressure, H1N1, HIV, AIDS, STD, arthritis, rheumatism, osteoporosis, and fibromyalgia, lung problems such as respiratory, asthma, tuberculosis, fungus on the lung, obesity, overweight, eating disorders, liver problems, hepatitis C, stomach problems, H.I. Polari, headaches, migraines, and blood clots, such as aneurisms in the brain and stomach, epilepsy (seizures), co-morbial conditions, Crohn's disease, gout, staff bacterial infections, infections, blindness, skin problems, eczema, allergies, food allergies, side effects from taking prescription drugs for illnesses that cause vision problems (seeing darkness), pain, menstrual cramps, miscarriages, deep lacerations, and fractures (Health Director, Healers', Health Professionals', Clients' Interviews 2010).

The Health Director ranks the top three most serious illnesses in the Seven First Nations and the Indian Friendship Centre as being diabetes, addictions, and poor mental health. The solutions that the Health Director recommends include becoming more active, less smoking with more smoking cessation strategies, diet, proper food consumption, and not avoiding but eating less of foods that are not healthy (Personal Interview May 20, 2010).

The reasons for the health issues include limited family doctors, family violence, teenage pregnancy issues, housing issues, literacy issues, poverty issues, healing lodge issues (closure), and educational issues. Limited knowledge, limited awareness, limited prevention programs, and limited or poor water resources contribute to the problems (Client Surveys 2010). The numerous health issues facing indigenous peoples are caused from the countless struggles and tribulations that they have been faced with since the onset of colonialism as far back as 500 years ago. The restraints and conflicts that indigenous peoples faced during colonialism are still relevant today. The lack of support from the government resonates just as strongly today as it did in the past. The government took away their traditions, culture, and languages, and forced the people to practice underground for fear of the loss of their way of life. The underground practices are known to continue even today. Now indigenous peoples struggle to regain and embrace their way of life without government support, when those very issues were caused by the government, "the ones who took it away."

---

to lack of oxygen when the blood flow to the brain is impaired by a blockage or rupture of an artery to the brain. A CVA is also referred to as a stroke (Medterms 2010).

The Integration of Traditional Medicine and Healers into the N'Mninoeyaa Aboriginal Health Access Centre
The Health Director's Perspective

The integration of traditional medicine and healers into Western clinics will require considerable cooperation from both parties in order to provide the best healthcare for patients. The Health Director thinks that traditional and Western medicine can work collaboratively with communication and bringing the two together. The integration will take the right type of traditional healer and practitioner, so that they hear and understand each other (Personal Interview May 20, 2010). One example that the Health Director used was an H1N1 manual developed by a traditional healer that included a lot of traditional medicines with contributions made by physicians. The health manual includes the proper dosage, preparation, and usage of traditional medicine.

In the N'Mninoeyaa Aboriginal Health Access Centre, the nurse practitioners make referrals to traditional healers, a step that has never been taken in the past. In working for an aboriginal First Nations organization, the nurse practitioners respect the fact that they treat aboriginal clients, and part of their knowledge base is to understand traditional healing. Traditional healing referrals by both the Native and non-Native nurse practitioners is a step forward toward integration, especially when a non-Native nurse practitioner makes more referrals than anyone else (Personal Interview May 20, 2010).

In-service training, which is well received by nurse practitioners, is a way in which the Health Centre is helping health practitioners to feel more comfortable in making referrals to a traditional healer. A traditional healer comes to the clinic and the clinic practitioners help with the building of a new teaching lodge and participate in the sweat lodge ceremony. The cultural teachings are preliminary, but have been occurring over a number of years. There have been five in-service training sessions to date. As part of the in-service training, a traditional healer brings practitioners on medicine walks. The nurse practitioners are given a working knowledge to help understand that traditional medicines react and help the body in just the same way Western medicines would. The Health Director said, "When I am doing workshops, I get someone to come in and discuss the properties of those plants so that they start saying, 'Oh yeah, that's right. I am doing the same thing as this traditional healer,' making the connection there. That is how I work with the practitioners. I know roughly what works and what doesn't. So I am trying to be basic on how we introduce it" (Personal Interview May 20, 2010).

A learning environment for all practitioners is fostered. Native practitioners bring their sacred pipes in and talk about their pipes. The North Shore Tribal Council integrates learning about traditional healing with little resistance.

Understanding First Nations peoples helps practitioners to make referrals with confidence in a traditional healing referral system. As an example of integrating traditional and Western medicines, the Health Director shared a story about a client who suffered from health problems associated with narcotic addictions. The Health Director said, "By using both systems, the healer and practitioner worked together to help the client rid himself of the narcotic addiction. Together, they actually work together; they are meeting with the client together. They are actually doing work together" (Personal Interview May 20, 2010).

In each community, the health centres determine where the healing is conducted by the healer. If a ceremony is needed, healers go and provide services if there is a healing lodge in their community. The healing can also be conducted in such places as the Powwow grounds (Personal Interview May 20, 2010).

Access to traditional healers and their helpers on a regular basis is very expensive. Traditional healers are the First Nations' specialists. The First Nations communities are fortunate to have healers in their communities every other month. The healer is accessed outside the health centre, and in the evenings, making house calls if needed. The healer accommodates the client's needs and will work wherever he/she is needed. There remains a concern for the limited healers that are available for the North Shore Tribal Council Health Centre. Traditional healer numbers are compared to, for instance, the limited number of heart specialists that are available. The Health Director says, "[Some] clients [still] have to travel to Toronto to seek a medical specialist who is knowledgeable, experienced, and skilled" (Personal Interview May 20, 2010).

The Health Centre funds some healing projects by providing resources, as well as some policies and procedures to ensure the best practices for the safety of the healer, the clients, and the tribal council. However, the Centre does not advise the communities which healer to bring in. The communities know which healers are comfortable and who works well in their community (Personal Interview May 20, 2010).

The inclination to visit either a traditional healer or a Western doctor is a matter of choice and upbringing. The health ethics of the Health Centre stress respect for personal choices. For instance, the Health Director's family members do not visit traditional healers, nor does the Director. They find the Health Centre more comfortable. Some clients are hesitant to visit a Western medicine clinic due to experiences that they have in the hospital. Some clients and community members still consider not having to visit an access centre a good thing. Health access is made available in their communities to better educate community members to understand that they should be taking care of their health every day. A funded traditional healing program was held and required an evaluation that presented some surprising results. The Health Director said, "They were surprised they just didn't go there for the medicine and stuff. They actually learned what health is all about and that it is about taking care of you, which is what traditional health has always emphasized. Contemporary health practitioners are now just getting into the importance of making sure they are doing a lot of that" (Personal Interview May 20, 2010).

The First Nations health benefits pay for the transportation for a healer to visit clients. There is funding from the Indian Residential School funding; there are dollars, but the Health Centre hopes for more funding, as it will take a lot more to achieve its goals. The Health Centre receives funding from a one-year pilot project but there is not enough. One healer comes in and serves about five or six communities. If the healer is servicing one community, community members can go and access the healer in another community. Funding is approximately $108,000 for all of the population, including the Indian Friendship Centre right down to Whitefish Lake. Just one community can ask for the $108,000. At present the government is willing to look at the way services are being offered, as traditional healing is being offered with less money. Community members would use it, validate it, and benefit from it, but there is not enough funding (Personal Interview May 20, 2010).

First Nations should develop a whole perspective on the integration of traditional medicine into Western clinics. The Health Director stated that health organizations have tried it over and over, along with NSTC and Chiefs' resolutions that demand more traditional incorporation. The policymakers at the government level have to make the difference. The Health Director says:

> First Nations can ground it in and do what we can do, but it has to work with the policy between provincial and federal levels of government. A policy that says traditional healers are recognized as similar to doctors. The government can only put money where there is policy. Otherwise they set the bar where everyone can get dollars and try to access dollars for everything. If that is the case we would all have a doctor in our community full time. It is the same thing; it does not work that way; the money is just not there. The politicians are responsible for working with the policymakers to help them understand that and make that happen. There should be a doctor once or twice a week; the communities would like at least a minimum of once a week in their communities. As far as the communities go, there are traditional healers but there is only $15,000 and the communities cost-share the dollars. Money is being spent on traditional healing, and they do what they can do,

but a health director is only a technician not, a politician (Personal Interview May 20, 2010).

First Nations use whatever resources they have by being creative with their funding. First Nations are under legal agreements the same as the North Shore Tribal Council Health Centre. Funding is not received to be able to just spend it the way they choose. The funding must be used as set in the legal agreement guidelines with no flexibility and mandatory reports submitted. First Nations meet their guidelines and use a very creative traditional approach so they can bring in more traditional healers. The Health Director stated, "I think it is just being creative at the traditional level, but by no means are they adequate" (Personal Interview May 20, 2010).

Health Professionals' Perspective

The Health professionals' survey results (n=13) from across the North Shores' Tribal Catchment area has provided critical information that is necessary to understanding the health issues in these communities. The knowledge and understanding of their perspectives on the possibilities of integrating traditional medicine and healers into Western clinics is significant to the research project.

The survey results show that health professionals support the integration of traditional medicine and healers into Western clinics. Most health professionals agreed that traditional medicine and healers are readily available for their clients, though their clients use them less than once a month. They noted improvements in clients' health after using traditional healing methods, but seven of the thirteen were unsure of the exact improvements (Health Professionals' Surveys 2010).

The majority of health professionals have at least some knowledge of traditional healing methods. On a scale of 1 to 7, the ratings varied, with four persons rating themselves a 4 (see figure below). The health professional who rated a 7 had a lot of knowledge, and is a recognized traditional healer/practitioner who conducts ceremonies for the communities. He worked extensively for the past fifteen years with healers who have more than thirty years of experience. The two practitioners who rated themselves a 6 referred to the Ojibwe culture healing circles; naming and spiritual clans; spiritual colors; Spring and Fall big drum ceremonies; healers/medicine persons; plants and teas; ceremonies; sweats and smudging; and dreams and intuition. Others who did not rate themselves mentioned the four sacred medicines and their uses; minigan (salve); spruce and balsam gum; red willow; frog leaves; and use of plants and herbs such as the blueberry root. One health professional mentioned the research she had undertaken during her professional training on the sweat lodge, shaking tent ceremonies, and some plant medicines (Health Professionals' Surveys 2010). There is a tremendous amount of traditional knowledge found in the survey results.

Health Professionals' Knowledge of
Traditional healing & ceremonial practices

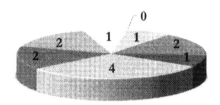

- Lot of knowledge (7)
- Some knowledge (6)
- More than average knowledge (5)
- Average knowledge (4)
- Below average knowledge (3)
- No knowledge (2, 1)
- No rating (0)

The majority of the health professionals (n=9) believe that traditional healing methods are effective. Five of the nine health professionals say they were led to believe in traditional healing methods. The belief came from visits with healers, Elders, upbringing, and individuals, or when they were children, their grandfathers treated all illnesses with natural medicines. One health professional said, "My grandmother practiced traditional healing using plants and herbs to treat medical conditions, for anxiety, pneumonia, and fluid retention/edema. Praying and smudging was used, but the healing was not called traditional healing. Being Catholic, we just thought it was normal" (Health Professionals' Surveys 2010). There is definite sign that not all traditional practices were lost, as the knowledge base is still quite connected to the people today. It is known that the traditional healing practices may have been saved by some of those people who went underground to practice their medicines and ceremonies in darkness, in order to practice their traditional way of life.

Four health professionals believe there is a relationship between Christianity and Native Spirituality. Four do not believe there is a relationship, and five are not sure. So at least nine of the thirteen health professionals do not believe, or are not sure, and one answered "no" to there being a relationship. Belief systems of the Anishinaabe reflect how spirituality plays an important role in healing. One health professional said, "I have experiences, and have witnessed clients who were deathly ill with cancer and were cured." Another referred to being raised in the Catholic Church as his family practiced many aspects of the Ojibwe culture, such as hunting, fishing, trapping, harvesting berries, herbs, and storytelling. He did not talk about being Aboriginal. As an adult, he saw many aspects of Christianity and Native Spirituality being similar. Another person based her knowledge on personal experience with ceremonies. Another health professional commented on Native Spirituality being tainted by Christianity (Health Professionals' Surveys 2010). If we consider the damage and repercussions that First Nations peoples were subjected to by assimilation and strict government regulations, Native people were not allowed to practice their culture and traditions, or speak their Native language, or practice traditional ceremonies and healing. We can justify the confusion, misinterpretations, lack of understanding, spirituality conflicts, and lack of or little belief in their own traditions.

The majority of health professionals agree that there is a need to teach First Nations peoples about traditional methods of healing. A suggestion that was made was to have the teachings be supported by all Chiefs and Councils. The health professionals chose the following to teach the community members the traditional methods of healing:

- Traditional healing methods by experiencing traditional healing
- Traditional teaching methods
- Traditional community awareness workshops by healers
- Traditional teachings for youth
- Traditional newsletters

Twelve of the thirteen health professionals recommend traditional healing methods to their clients. A health professional wrote, "It is usually upon enquiry, if the client is interested after an explanation, but it is not forced, as it is entirely up to the client." A suggestion that was noted was that "our people need to know it works" to better understand our ways of healing, and it works, and "it's our way." Other health professionals commented that traditional healing should be available as an option. Another health professional commented, "Traditional healing should be available, especially around some psychosocial issues; I feel that certain clients would benefit from seeing a traditional healer." In a health professional's assessment of her clients, she said, "With every client I see, as part of their intake assessment, I ask them if they have used traditional healing methods, and whether they would be interested in using them. I make referrals to local traditional healers, or the healer they have been using. Traditional healing is referred for some illnesses and conditions." Nine of thirteen agreed that their workplace health clinics engaged in traditional healing methods on site, and rated the traditional healing use at four to five, with seven being very frequent. Four of nine said that their workplace did not engage in traditional healing methods. Traditional healing is used in health clinics that are rated low to average use (Health Professionals' Surveys 2010).

Reasons for illnesses that relate to the physical, social, mental & spiritual aspects of health
Health Professionals - 13 Surveys

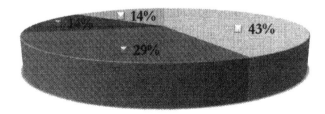

14%   14%   43%   29%

᛫ Lack of funding for traditional healing

᛫ Racism, Mobility, Lack of housing, Poverty level, Lack of educational opportunities to improve aboriginal lifestyle

᛫ Smoking, Inactivity, Addiction issues (gambling, food), Sexual abuse, Elder abuse, Lack of funding for training/education, Lack of resources and knowledge about culture and traditional lifestyle, Loss of the extended family unit
᛫ Poor Access to medicine, equipment, personal support, home making, home maintenance, respite care particularly those without a family doctor, or those living with complex chronic medical conditions, Tobacco misuse, Diet

The Health Centre Clients' Perspective
Batchewana First Nation (Rankin), Garden River First
Nation, Indian Friendship Centre (Sault Ste. Marie)

The individuals who participated in the survey are clients of the Health Centre and provide fundamental feedback to support the integration of traditional medicine and healers into Western clinics.

There were twenty-three clients who were status Indians who participated in the survey. Sixteen lived on reserve and seven lived off reserve. Fourteen were females, of which nine were between the ages of 40 and 60, two were 20 to 40, and three were 60 plus. Most females rated their health to be between average (3) to perfect health (7). There were six males, of which five were between the ages of 20 and 40; one participant was under twenty. Males rated their health an average of 5. The average income was $12,000 to $35,000, with seven people who fit that salary range and three people who made a salary of $20,000 to $35,000, and one person who made below $12,000. There were no salaries over $50,000, and four participants did not answer the question (Client Surveys 2010). The health of First Nations peoples is seen within the survey results; the low income base reflects on the lifestyle of the participants, and the location is mostly on reserve, where there are more poverty and health issues.

The survey participants included three participants who were 60 years old or older, and rated their health a 5, on a scale of 1 to 7, with 7 being excellent health, and one noted her health issues as pernicious anemia and osteoporosis. Nine participants in the 40 to 60 age groups rated their health between 3 and 7. Remarks included pain in the body to perfect health. Two people in the 20 to 40 age group rated their health a 5. Two participants did not answer the demographic information (Client Surveys 2010). Health issues such as diabetes, cancer, heart disease, asthma, COPD, heart problems, high blood pressure, serious illness, pernicious anemia, osteoporosis, and pain in the body were listed (Client Surveys 2010). When we consider the health issues mentioned and how participants rated their health as fairly good, there is somewhat of a conflict that arises. Is it because they feel good about their lives in other aspects rather than focusing on their ailments when they rated their health? Is their emotional, spiritual, and mental health good, and they work at the physical maintenance of their health in order to have a balanced way of life?

Sixteen of the twenty-two responders visit traditional healers for their health problems. Clients understand traditional healing methods and are aware of traditional healing methods through family ties to traditional remedies. Most clients follow their traditional ways of life, and prefer to visit both a Western doctor and a traditional healer (Client Surveys 2010). The norm is to visit a Western doctor along with a traditional doctor to address health issues, but many do not share this information with their Western doctors for fear of ridicule and the Western mind-set of disbelief toward traditional healing practices. The healers share their gifts to cure their people, as it is the Creator's making of the natural world that healers work in, work with, and work for the betterment of people.

Culture and tradition are defined in the context of spirituality. Clients were asked if there was a difference between spiritual healing and traditional healing but were unsure of the difference. Some clients agree that there is no relationship between Christianity and Native Spirituality, and only a few agree that there is a relationship (Client Surveys 2010).

Clients agreed that traditional and Western medicine can be integrated, and that it is a good idea to integrate it. Fifty percent of the clients rated the integration an excellent idea. Most clients agreed that educational workshops on traditional healing are a good idea. Community awareness workshops, traditional teaching methods, and experiencing the traditional healing were rated average to high. Few clients agreed that their First Nation health clinic engaged in traditional healing methods on site, some were not sure, and a few disagreed that traditional healing methods were used by their First Nation. Most clients agreed that traditional healing was not recommended to them by Western medical clinics (Client Surveys 2010). The integration opportunities to engage in cultural teachings are obvious and much needed in the communities so that people understand, and will embrace their ways of life more readily without fear.

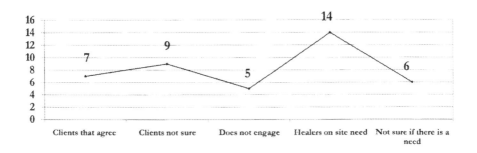

Do First Nations Health Clinics engage in Traditional Healing Methods On Site?
Is there a need to have Traditional Healers on site?
22 - Survey Clients

Client Survey Results on the Integration of
Traditional & Western Medicine
Survey Clients - 22

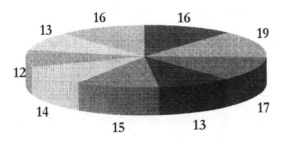

16   16
13   19

12

14   17
15   13

* Visit Healers

* Would visit a healer

* Healers help them

* Traditional healing is not
recommended

* Understand healing methods

* Prefer both a Traditional
Healer & Western doctor

* Awareness from family ties

Follow their traditional way of
life

* Believe in Traditional medicine
& healers methods of healing

**Strategies to increase access to Traditional Healers & The
Traditional Healing Role in overcoming health problems
Survey Clients - 22**

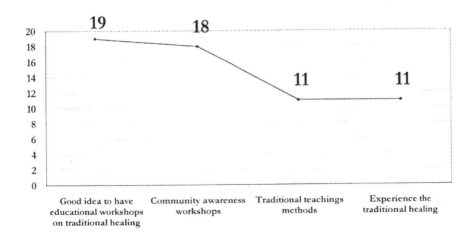

19   18

11   11

Good idea to have	Community awareness	Traditional teachings	Experience the
educational workshops	workshops	methods	traditional healing
on traditional healing			

The Perspective of Healers' Clients

Clients who heal and feel better have provided their experiences of better health after healing and the medicines they are given in the following stories:

Francine said that seeing Tom helped her quite a lot: "I could not lift my hands up before; now I can." Francine talked about the time she was put in the hospital and did not know what was going on during that time. She said, "When I got out, I went and saw Tom, and ever since then I have been feeling good. So I have to keep taking it like he said every six months." Francine mentioned that she quit taking the medicine the Western doctor gave her because "I am getting sick." She told her doctor she would see her own traditional healer. She said, "Since I have been seeing him I have been doing pretty good." The Western doctor did not like that she was visiting a traditional medicine person for her health problems. John, her husband, said, "He was speechless." When I asked Francine how the natural medicine from the healer is working for her, Francine said, "It is really working." Francine's illnesses include diabetes, fibromyalgia, rheumatism, arthritis, and heart problems (Client Interviews 2010).

John referenced a story about another healer who helped a man avoid getting his leg amputated. The healer asked the man to wait for five or six days before going back to the doctor. He said his leg would clear up. The man had an infection in his leg from bad circulation. The food he was eating was bad, so she told him, "You will eat what I cook for the next six days, eat nothing else." Just following that advice cleared up his leg infection (Client Interviews 2010).

Hope said the treatment she experienced from the healer Francis has helped. She said, "It has given me an understanding of why things happened in terms of health-related problems. Has it cured actual physical ailments? Absolutely yes, that has happened. It gives me some teachings about the underlying issues that result from those physical health problems" (Client Interviews 2010).

Hope uses traditional healers quite often for her health needs, but she also visits her Western doctor whom she informs of her traditional healing use. She thinks that traditional medicine and Western medicine can work cooperatively, but she does not think that a Western doctor should practice traditional medicine at the same time (Client Interviews 2010).

Hope says, "The best way to know the right healer to visit is largely through word of mouth—when people say they are cured, or that they are really doing well; but the relationship that you build with your healer may not be good for me"(Client Interviews 2010).

The Traditional Healers' Perspective

It was important to interview healers to gain insight into the methods of healing, the illnesses that they cure, the medicines they use, their holistic views on the integration processes, and how the problems and solutions they find evolve within their communities internally and externally when they are faced with the serious health issues of their First Nations peoples.

Integration in Hospitals

One of the recommendations that Tom made was that he would like to see Western health professionals use traditional medicine intravenously. Tom said, "I would think it would work a lot better if it goes into intravenous because it would go right into the veins, and it would go all over. Yeah it filters as it gets into the organ parts, but the other way it would go all over. That way it would probably cure people with three or four jugs [Tom measures traditional medicine in "jugs."] maybe in two weeks" (Healer Interviews 2010).

Tom talked about working with people in hospitals in the United States, and he said, "They allow it over there." Tom explained that they refrigerate the medicine that he makes for him, and they give the patient the glass of medicine three times a day, "whatever I ask." Tom also said that a woman doctor he does not know refers a lot of people to him through the Wellness Centre, and the Wellness Centre sends them to his residence. Other places, like the Cheboygan, Michigan hospital, which does not allow traditional medicine, claim that there is too much red tape to have it approved. A doctor called Tom and told him it was not approved, or certified, for the hospital, but he was allowed to bring it into a senior facility, because there was no law that prohibited traditional medicine use (Healer Interviews 2010).

Mabel explains a way in which to integrate traditional and Western methods with a healing experience: "A Native man was having his leg amputated and they could have gone above the blanket with the wash cloth at that time. If the doctors had the knowledge of the cedar bath ceremony, and why that individual needed that ceremony, they could incorporate it, and allow that to happen. The doctor could assess him and find out what his statistics are, what his blood pressure is at, what his mentality is, and what if, during the cedar bath, he wants to release that emotion." Cross-cultural teachings are necessary to implement traditional healing for Native patients so that the patients can receive the best care during their surgeries (Healer Interviews 2010).

Leonard noted that there were difficulties in the past when they would go into the hospitals to smudge people who were going to pass away. "Now we just say to the hospital that we are there to smudge a person, and they tell us where to go, and we go and do it. We use a light smudge because it is a hospital. We compromise for conditions. They are more open to it. Some people come up and give compliments, and say, I wish they would do this to all the patients. One person said that they don't really see the doctors. One family needed to, and wanted a spirit name for the person that was passing away. We did not smoke the pipe, but we did singing and smudging" (Healer Interviews 2010).

The healer Francis said, "One way of integrating in a non-Native setting is a way we can get our work done; it still is not Native, it is with forms and records, and it is kind of combining both things, but it is not really our way. It's a means to get it. We've been in this hospital since 1996; then I came in 1999. We were the first ones to incorporate" (Healer Interviews 2010).

Integrating Western and Traditional Doctors and Practitioners

Mabel spoke about the healing lodge being the vision of her father-in-law and said that contemporary and traditional people needed to start working together. Contemporary should not be over and above traditional, and traditional should not be over and above contemporary, but they need to work together to do the healing work. She said, "They could have started doing more of their research work on how traditional medicine would work with some people. Where they have a choice, they have a choice to choose traditional medicine versus contemporary medicine. It is important if you are going to integrate that you can still work together. A doctor and traditional medicine person can start working jointly on the patient, and reviewing the analysis together, and reporting and keeping the records on how. A traditional clinic would be when Francis comes in, and we are using the sacred fire, tobacco, and the traditional ceremonies with the drum" (Healer Interviews 2010).

Integration is beneficial for curing narcotic addiction when a traditional healer and a physician work side by side. The client is helped by both systems working together to help the client rid himself of the addiction. Both traditional and Western methods make a difference from the point of view of the client (Personal Interview May 20, 2010).

Mabel mentioned a nurse practitioner that has a little machine for testing medicines. For instance, if someone is taking high blood pressure pills and wants traditional medicine, they use this mechanism to see if certain traditional medicines will interact with one another—or with the Western medicine. "You can type into the mechanism what prescription they are on, and then you take whatever research has been done in regard to a certain plant's ingredients to find out how that plant will interact with the prescribed high blood pressure pill" (Healer Interviews 2010).

Mabel says, "Other health centres' tribulations can be used to repair or fix ours. Even to bring our own people up to the level of acceptance. People can have a choice, and have that respect for traditional medicine, and the storage of traditional medicine at the same level as you would store and hold Western medicine, in a respectful way, instead of storing it whatever" (Healer Interview 2010).

Mabel shared a story about a workshop she attended by a Chinese doctor who had studied traditional medicine and its effect on people's health. In particular, he showed diabetic feet and how they could be healed. The ulcers could be healed because he knew how to drain them. Western and traditional methods can work together when assisting diabetic patients with diabetic foot problems, by sharing medical information (Healer Interviews 2010).

Bill said, "In order to integrate, you have to educate. I would say let the traditional medicine man or woman work with a doctor for about a year, and then have that doctor work under that traditional medicine man as well. Let them work together, how would you say, combine the two. Why can't a doctor ask for an opinion on this client, and the traditional medicine man says maybe this root can help him, or that is fine, let's give him that instead? I do not believe in radiation for cancer, because to me it is like sticking your head in a microwave" (Healer Interviews 2010).

Many health professionals respect the fact that they work and treat aboriginal patients in an aboriginal organization. Health professionals need to have the knowledge base to understand traditional medicine and healing. Some nurse practitioners make referrals to traditional medicine people (Personal Interview May 20, 2010).

Mabel said, "The natural medicines in their natural form can do a lot of healing work for the people, and if Western medicine worked together [with natural medicines], they could do the analysis on how that progression would be. If they supported one another, and worked together, they could be doing that research instead of paying research companies to do the research. They would be able to do hands-on research with finding cures with natural medicine" (Healer Interviews 2010).

Lillie mentioned that "if doctors and nurses understood a traditional person, and healers are not going in and doing bad things with the devil, or whatever, I believe the integration would be good. The healing is just what we were given to work. We can work together; they do their thing, and everybody else does their thing, and we can work together, not run each other down, I will say. The continuity of spirits, when you deal with the spiritual, the physical comes up, and I don't deal with the physical, I work with it but the doctor knows what needs to be done. Maybe there is a pill that they need. My gosh, it would be so awesome" (Healer Interviews 2010).

For integration of traditional and Western practices, Tom said, "I would not be able to examine the client. They would just have to tell me what, and then I would have to get them to get a slip from a doctor that gets them checked over to tell him what's wrong, and then I could … then I can treat them." Tom referenced his own healing one fall when he felt dizzy and was going to pass out. He had left his sister's home feeling dizzy, and fell to the ground. His sister insisted he go to the Western doctor. He was given pills, which he did not take; instead he asked his brother-in-law to make him a tea out of birch buds, cut to a certain length, which solved his problem (Healer Interviews 2010).

THE FOUR ASPECTS OF THE
INTEGRATION MODEL

I n order to integrate, we should consider the four aspects of the integration model of traditional healing and Western practices. These can be compared to a person's life, as in the four directions, the four colors, the balanced way of life that are symbolic of the physical, mental, emotional, and spiritual aspects of human life.

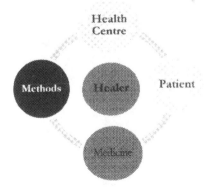

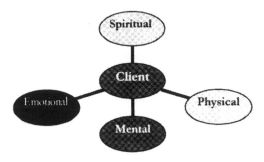

Four Aspects of the Medicine Wheel for the Client

Funding

Mabel suggests that "Health Canada themselves become cross-culturally trained because they are the ones holding the purse strings. If Health Canada has no concept of what is viable for traditional health, then how are they going to be approving things? They may be cutting things that are desperately needed, such as ceremonial practices. How do you bring in and accept what traditional is all about?" There is a difference in the components that the traditional medicine person would have that the Western doctor is not going to have with that medicine. Mabel thinks that integrating traditional and Western medicines would be an excellent opportunity for the health and well-being of people (Healer Interviews 2010).

Funding is critical in strategizing to increase the integration of traditional medicine and healers with Western clinics. The strategy will help to increase the client's use of healers by making the healers more readily available. At present, the First Nations' health benefits pay for the transportation costs of having a healer come. The Health Director said, "There are Indian Residential School dollars, and we are hoping that there are more dollars because it takes a lot more" (Personal Interview May 20, 2010).

Funding traditional healers on a regular basis would help to increase access to healers by making them readily available for clients. Traditional healers are specialists and cost money. Accessibility varies when using traditional healers—they work in the evenings, and they make house calls. Healers will attend to their clients at their residences, or wherever the healing needs to be carried out (Healer Interviews 2010).

Policies and Procedures

The healer Francis says, "Health Canada actually needs to let Anishinaabe people set it up the way it needs to be, so we have a trade off there. We set this up in a way so that we knew that traditional would work in this clinic. Set it up that way, and they in turn have their rules and regulations. We have locks on all of our cabinets, and we document everything that is the trade-off. We can do our Anishinaabe ceremonies, we do what they want, and we write our total records in Anishinaabe. We understand and say to each other what we are doing" (Healer Interviews 2010).

Mabel adds, "The traditional health program developed policies and procedures based on Western society's concepts. We have grown to develop safety mechanisms where, let's say, you are going into a sweat and that conductor says, 'Okay, you need to take all your clothes off, and get in there with me all by yourself.' The teachings say that you do not do that. Now you have to have an individual that if you are going to see a healer you have a helper there, too. The healer cannot create anything wrong with the patient, and the patient cannot create anything wrong with the healer" (Healer Interview 2010).

Education, Training and Apprenticeship

Mabel says, "If you are going to incorporate traditional and contemporary, there are a lot of ceremonies we could do. Mabel suggests cross-cultural teachings in order for health professionals to understand why we need to do a cedar bath ceremony for someone who just went through surgery. "When you cut the energy force, there is a leakage that you cannot physically see but spiritually you can see. When you put that medicine on there, that cedar medicine, it kind of repairs that" (Healer Interviews 2010).

Lillie suggests getting the young people to attend circles and she holds circles every second Monday. She says, "Even when we had it once a week a long time ago, the kids were starting to come" (Healer Interviews 2010).

Lillie mentions that they talked about having a gathering with people who work with medicine. "A lady from Quebec and one from Timmins, and between the two of them there is over 100 years of experience in traditional medicine. If this is possible with just a few knowledgeable people, there must be many more healers that may be accessible" (Healer Interviews 2010).

Lillie's helper Maggie suggests a coming together of those Elders who are in the helping field so all people have access. She says, "The work they are doing is the gathering of the young and old to learn about the gifts that everyone carries. There would be knowledge shared about other peoples' gifts, and a connection with others, and information would be shared about healing practices. They are all open to it" (Healer Interviews 2010).

Mabel says, "They need to do this (integrate) to take the burden off the health care system. Even though they will pay out first to get those healers to be on-site healers, it is going to relieve the health care system in the long term. It will cut the costs of it. If Francis came in once a month to work with people, if you want to start off by doing some research work, say we bring him in once a quarter. He was coming in once a month, when he needed to see people again. The needs have been consistent, and depending on their illnesses, require more. If Francis came in twice a month, one portion of his visits could be set aside for apprenticeship training by the healer. When they made the treaties, the government said that you have the medicine chest to support the medicine chest, all the resources that the Western society got from this land is their payment to cover that medicine chest. Whatever it took to cover the medicine chest, well now that medicine chest can support traditional healers in doing the healing work" (Healer Interviews 2010).

Francis mentioned that he tried to start an apprenticeship. He said, "It is a special person, and just about everybody I tried to start to apprentice gets this big swollen head, and gets half cocked, and gets a stupid head and challenges me. I had about ten people and even my nephew gets pissed off with me, and I don't even know why, mainly. I worked with my mentor forever. Young people don't have that kind of commitment. It takes certain knowledge of God-given natural born ability, natural spirit ability, not everybody can heal" (Healer Interviews 2010).

He continues, "I hear people talk about how they have healed and what happened, and what people did for them all over." Talking about their healing experience is a way in which to increase client access to healers (Healer Interviews 2010).

It is a gift to heal, from the perspective of the healer Francis, who says, "You know, the people know me wherever I go; even with people I don't know, or even with different tribes somebody recognizes that within me. If I do not know them, they have an inner understanding; it has happened to me over and over. No matter where I go—California, Louisiana, Saskatchewan, and Alberta—people will just come up and say, 'I don't know but I know you can help me with this.' We start talking, and they have no idea what I do around here even. So I think the spirits define that, and the people do. When I began, I was just doing it to help people, and to help my elders." Francis was content just helping his elders, getting the medicines, and preparing for the ceremonies. Today, he sees medicine men that are healers that don't do things for themselves anymore. "They get a big throne, and get everybody to do that [their work]. I don't; if there is a sweat to be done; I am out there making fire, and helping with the medicine. I don't sit around and not participate. That is where I came from, and I am not too far away from where I came. I have been to the NSTC area, Minnesota, Wisconsin, Ontario, over by Kenora, down in Iowa, and over in Saskatchewan. Diabetes is the number-one starter of everything we have, even the cancers and heart problems, kidney problems and those kinds of things. Diabetes-related issues are the number one for our people, so that is what I deal with lots" (Healer Interviews 2010).

Mabel tells her story about her father-in law's vision of the healing lodge. "The healing vision was to have contemporary and traditional medicine people working together to heal people. The vision of that is holistic in the healing lodge, and those teachings about the sacred fire needing to be there. About those four doorways, and all who come to seek healing are to be welcomed. If someone needed to come and seek healing, or who needed that family structure and support, he'd be welcome there. That different people heal at different rates, so you can't pinpoint if you are going to stay there for four weeks and receive this traditional healing medicine. It has to be four weeks for this person, or six weeks, or two weeks for that person, or whatever. The research work would happen if they worked together in charting the well-being of people in what is working with one individual, and what is not working for the people. They would be able to do their research work in that way, but not to patent the medicine. That would be a destructive thing, and that would not work between contemporary and traditional medicine people. They need to start working together. It would be an excellent opportunity for the health and well-being of people. They could have that choice; right now people don't have that choice." Mabel's father-in-law cured people with cancer. The doctor wanted to put it in the system to make money. The doctor wanted to develop that medicine. But her father-in-law said, "It will never work for you, it's that spiritual relationship, and you can't give it to them because they don't have that" (Healer Interviews 2010).

Bill talks about "the traditional medical centre in the States being a part of their Western medicine. I think myself, we should incorporate it here. There is no reason why we can't go and have traditional medicine within our community rather than going out, or bringing somebody in. If there is a person in your community who makes traditional medicine, why can't we be supplied with it at the health centres? We have a clinic once or twice a week. We have Western medicine coming in once a week. Why can't we have our medicine people? You could have your clinics down there once or twice a week." Bill goes on to say, "First thing we have to do is educate ourselves on what a vision is. Like my dad fasted for ten days, he went without food and water to get that vision of the lodge. I think that you would not have the abuse we see today in prescription drugs, because the traditional medicine does not have any chemicals in it. Secondly, it would probably be safer for our children. If you take a pill and you put it down and that child takes it, it's going to affect [the child]. If you take cedar tea and put it there, and let that child drink it, it will not do any damage. It will benefit our people to be safer, and it will benefit our people to be readily available, and it will benefit our people to get back to that way of life again" (Healer Interviews 2010).

Bill says, "Traditional medicine is handed down from family to family. I think that has to be recognized; if it takes a piece of paper, then let's give the paper out. My dad, he had grade 3, but he had an honorary doctor's degree because of the medicine he made" (Healer Interviews 2010).

Francis referenced better education on food consumption for diabetics. He said, "Diabetes is controlled by food and diet. Foods that are in the European diet are real foreign to our bodies—the white sugars, the white flours, and processed foods. We are looking at hundreds of thousands of years of natural eating, eating natural plants and animals from Mother Earth that we take from what the Great Spirit put here for us. This used to be our diet. We never had diabetes before when we focused on just a Native diet. All these sweets and sugars seem to be what our people focus on nowadays. Diet would be the number-one thing at a really young age, and appropriate control of it in our homes and stores. When you go to a Native feast now, you look at what is there. There may be a little bit of wild game and berries. Look at the mac and cheese, spam, fry bread—you know all these things that are really terrible for our body ... Our Native diet consists of wild roots, wild berries, wild game, fish, ducks, geese, and wild turkeys. Those kinds of things, that kind of game that was given to us were all of our foods. All this other stuff that we have come to understand as the Indian diet [was] what we were forced to eat in order to survive" (Healer Interviews 2010).

Tom reflects that people used to be healthy in his community. They had their own water from their own wells, and they grew their own gardens (Healer Interviews 2010).

Healers Who Heal the People

Tom said to a man with a heart problem, "You have to take this medicine." The man said, "No, I don't believe in it." Tom said, "Well then you are going to have to have that triple heart bypass that the doctor told you about. So his daughter came in and I said make sure he drinks a cup every day; put that in a pot and drink it. He drank it for three days; he went up and got tested, and the doctor said, 'I don't know what you are doing, but you don't need your triple bypass' " (Healer Interviews 2010).

Another person who had tumors in his lungs was treated with traditional medicine by Tom. Gilles, the client of the healer, sent a letter to Tom that I read. He said, "Miigwetch, your medicine seems to work. I had an X-ray and nothing showed in my lungs." Tom actually shipped the medicine to him in Quebec. Another example was with a young thirteen-year-old boy and his parents who came to visit Tom. The parents told Tom that their son had only three weeks to three months to live. Tom's says, "I said the problem with those goddamn doctors is they give you this for that, that for that, and nothing is working. They don't know a damn thing."

The mother said, "I am a doctor."

Tom asked her, "How come you don't treat your boy?"

She said, "You can't do that in the States."

Tom received a call from the boy's mother, the doctor, and she told him that her son drank all the medicine on the way back home. Tom said, "If you have a cold, do you drink the whole bottle of medicine all at once?" The boy drank all the medicine on the way back home, which was meant to be drunk over a period of time to help cure the cancer (Healer Interviews 2010).

Tom has cured many people, such as a woman with lumps in her breast. The sick woman visited Tom, crying; she was dying from cancer. The woman drank four jugs of his cancer medicine, and in a month there was no sign of cancer. She was being treated by a cancer doctor. Another woman had a blood clot with one clot close to her brain. The Western doctors could not take one of the clots out; she was a walking time bomb. She drank Tom's medicine, and as Tom explains it, "She goes to bingo everyday." Tom talked about a man who had an aneurism in his stomach, but chose to use Western medicine to have the aneurism removed. He said, "All he had to do is drink that medicine for three or four days, and it would have cleared that all out" (Healer Interviews 2010).

Tom talked about his great aunt on his wife's side of the family who had high blood pressure. He told her that she would have to give up her pills. Her answer was, "No sir, no sir. I am not giving up my pills."

He said, "No use me making the medicine, because it won't work."

One day, after it had snowed; his mother-in-law asked Tom to make the medicine because she was so dizzy. He shoveled under the snow, digging down and getting as much wintergreen as he could. He put it in a pot, and she drank it. She went to the doctor, and the doctor told her she did not need to take any more pills; her blood pressure was normal. She said she was going to take her pills anyway; she took them for sixty years. She is still alive today in her late nineties (Healer Interviews 2010).

Tom has cured people with gout, asthma, and eczema. He said gout is cured within two to three treatments. Tom talks about his own mishap, when he was cut badly with an axe, right to the bone. He took gum off a tree with a leaf and covered his wound. The next morning he took it off, and the wound was sore, but it was healed. He could hardly see anything. He said, "That is when I said that can cure cancer" (Healer Interviews 2010).

Another healer who travels around to heal people, Francis, healed a woman from Toronto who had a tumor in the centre of her upper brain that was inoperable, and about the size of a golf ball. He says, "She came to us and we worked on her. She asked if I would look after her when she went to have her surgery. She said, 'Will you look after me when I am in there?' I said I would do what I could, and I did the ceremony for her." When she told her white doctor who she was visiting, the doctor told her, "Hocus pocus," and said that it wouldn't work and the woman needed to stay with the Western doctors. She went back to the hospital to get her head checked, and they took a new X-ray scan. They came back and got her again, and did another X-ray from the back, and then from all sides of her head. She asked them why they needed all the X-rays and they showed her the X-ray and CAT scan from two or three weeks before, when the tumor was as big as a golf ball. The one they were doing that morning, they said, showed that it was less than the size of a dime, and she said, "That must be that hocus pocus" (Healer Interviews 2010).

Francis remembers a time in his life that the spirits told him not to doctor for two months. He personally did not want to stop doctoring, especially when a mother brought her small child to him for healing. She did not bring him simaa[26] (tobacco). Francis could see the child's tumor in her head, and he knew he could get it out. The people wanted a ceremony, but he could not offer it at that time. Francis said, "The day the child was admitted, as soon as the day, it was in my head that whole time, I did it" (Healer Interviews 2010).

Francis talks about one man who was referred to him by Western doctors. "His cholesterol was up to 800, and they were having fits because they knew he was going to stroke out or die soon. This was just last year. They tried everything they had; in 3 months we had his cholesterol down to 300" (Healer Interviews 2010).

Healing can be in the form of going out and picking medicine, as Leonard says: "You are outdoors; you are breathing clean air; it is healing in itself. The healing part is connecting to the medicine." Leonard says that traditional medicine has been helping, as people have been getting cancer, doctors give up, and people have been getting traditional medicine for conditions from warts to cancer. When asked if it is improving their health, Leonard answers emphatically, "Yes" (Healer Interviews 2010).

Leonard, who conducts sweat lodges, says, "We go in and smudge people

---

26 Simaa, one of the four sacred medicines offered to traditional people for help in healing or for answers.

in the hospital. We just go in when they need you, I guess. In order to integrate, he sees conflicts in the integration, but at the same time they both need to bend a bit in order to work together (Healer Interviews 2010).

Bill speaks of a father who was trying to help his son to stop drinking. At the sweat lodge ceremony the son did not show up. Bill insisted that they go and get the boy so he could attend the ceremony meant for his healing. Bill brought him there while he had been drinking, and, Bill says, "It actually helped him" (Healer Interviews 2010).

Barriers to the Integration of Traditional Medicine and Healers into Western Clinics
The Health Director's Perspective

According to the Health Director, the biggest factor that deters the integration of traditional medicine and healers with Western medicine is the lack of funding. The North Shore Tribal Council Health Centre (NSTCHC) does not have adequate resources to be fully integrated with Western and traditional medicine. Additionally, many funding sources do not recognize traditional healing as legitimate. The Health Director says, "It is easier for me to get money for another doctor than it is for a traditional healer. It's just the way our system went up; we constantly put in proposals, and we constantly require the need. Maybe we will make it there eventually." Proposals are being submitted regularly to accommodate the need, with the hope that eventually they will be able to accommodate the traditional needs. The Health Director says, "Health organizations have tried it over and over. Planning, Tribal Council, and Chiefs' resolutions demanding more traditional medicine and healers have not been addressed. It is the policymakers at the government level that have to make the difference. We can ground it in and we can do what we can do, but it has to work with the policy. There needs to be a policy at the provincial and federal levels that says that traditional healers are recognized as similar to doctors" (Personal Interview May 20, 2010).

Another barrier, according to the health director, is the lack of traditional healers. She describes the shortage of healers as similar to a shortage in specialists. When a medical practitioner refers a client to see a traditional healer, and there is no healer available for a couple of months, this is a barrier to integrating the two medical systems (Personal Interview May 20, 2010).

The Health Professionals' Perspective

Ten out of thirteen health professionals use traditional healing methods and recommend that healers be available on-site regularly, yet there are still barriers to integration. According to the health professionals, the major barriers to integrating traditional medicine and healers into Western clinics are:

- Lack of knowledge of aboriginal culture and issues
- Lack of interest by community members
- Lack of exposure
- Lack of opportunity to learn about traditional healing
- Lack of a process for integrating traditional healing into Western practices
- Reluctance to be seen as "quacks" by their Western colleagues
- Lack of planning
- Lack of training of healers
- Lack of consistency in training of healers
- Lack of identification of aboriginal clients within their Western practices
- Lack of traditional healers
- Lack of transportation

(Health Professionals' Surveys 2010)

Perhaps the most significant barrier is the need for people to better understand indigenous culture and tradition, including indigenous healing. Interestingly, their comments include a discussion on the different viewpoints of those raised in Catholic households versus more traditional households. The participants noted that Catholic individuals may see traditional medicine as being at odds with the traditional teachings of the Roman Catholic Church. Individuals who attended residential school may be unaware of traditional teachings and healings, as they have not had exposure to traditional healers. Many families have lost much of their cultural teachings and use of traditional medicines because their parents were raised in residential schools. This shows the need for more traditional teachings that are conducted by genuine traditional healers and knowledgeable elders who understand their teachings, in order to educate others in the traditional way of life. The culture and traditions are what is needed to bring the indigenous peoples back to what they lost after being subjects of assimilation processes. The awareness will help community members understand and embrace traditional healing practices and overcome barriers that can help them to heal and live healthier lives.

The Traditional Healers' Perspectives

The following are reflections on the barriers that First Nations healers view as preventing them from working side by side within Western clinics, using holistic and traditional ways of healing that are ancient medicinal practices passed on from generation to generation.

The barriers to the integration of traditional and Western practices that healers note include:

- Fear of the possibility of government-enforced laws for treating sick people, and repercussions such as jail if something should go wrong.

    - A barrier that arose for a healer, Tom, was when he was going to make cancer medicine for a woman the day he cut his arm with the axe. He was told that if he made the medicine for her and she died, he would go to jail. So he did not make anything for her for fear of the repercussions. Tom says, "It would probably be the government that would stop it, if the government passed a law that said you can't make any medicine" (Healer Interviews 2010).

- Closing a traditional lodge presents fewer opportunities to draw healers, to find healing, and to receive answers from traditional ceremonies with sacred fires.

    - The closing of a traditional lodge has had a tremendous effect on the well-being of Native people in one of the First Nations. Mabel speaks about what people got from the sacred fire, and how that sacred fire drew a certain healer, and how things were said that helped each individual. Mabel says, "It's the spirit of the people, and of that sacred fire that draws the answers. Then that answer comes to the individual through whatever might happen in the circle; that's why you can never say that anyone is greater than, or less than [another]. Everyone has something to contribute in the circle that may help someone else. We don't know who is being helped by whatever" (Healer Interviews 2010).

    - There are no operational dollars to operate the healing lodge. Mabel says the health system has to cut back on their expenses. If they had traditional medicine people doing that doctoring work for the people, and teaching them how to look after themselves, too, they would be cutting, but they have vested interests. "Pharmacies and doctors have shares in pharmaceuticals, and all those big industries want money; they keep society trapped" (Healers Interviews 2010).

- People do not believe that traditional medicines and healers can heal sickness.

    - Lack of belief is a huge factor that could deter the integration. Tom realizes that some people don't believe. Tom's own brother-in-law, who had a cancer tumor in his heart, would not drink the medicine that Tom brought to him (Healer Interviews 2010).

- Some doctors refuse to treat patients when they become aware of traditional healing choices the patients have made.

    - Mabel tells of a long-time resident of her community who had cancer. She says, "The cancer patient divulged to her doctor that she wanted to take traditional medicine but also wanted her doctor to care for her. The doctor did not want to work with her anymore, because she chose traditional medicine versus what the doctor wanted to prescribe. If Western and traditional started to work together, they could have worked with the patient and seen how that medicine was going to work with her" (Healer Interviews 2010).

- In order to incorporate, patient records need to be kept together.

    - Mabel discusses keeping patient records. She says, "At present, traditional files are kept separate from the regular client files. If they are going to incorporate both here they would keep both of those records together" (Healer Interviews 2010).

- Traditional healing will affect Western practices if more people are healed.

    - Tom says, "If we start healing a lot of people we are going to do them out of business. That is why they keep them right to the last minute when they've got cancer, and then they send them here when they can't do nothing for them" (Healer Interviews 2010).

- There are limited numbers of genuine healers, as there are many scammers who say they are authentic healers.

    - Healers share the concern of other research participants in that there are a limited number of authentic traditional medicine people. Tom says, "There are a lot of scammers that say they are genuine healers." How does one determine who is a true healer? Comments include "Healers should not ask you for money up front," "Use your own intuition," and, "Ask if they have ever healed anyone (Healer Interviews 2010).

- Without the proper knowledge of traditional healers and medicine, sick people reach out for help from bogus healers.

  - Lillie and her helper Maggie mention that "there are so many coming up, and telling people to come this way, come this way. The people who don't have the traditional knowledge are trying to get help, so they will reach out to anywhere, and there is a lot out there. The bogus healers present difficulties for sick people when people in need of traditional healing become victims of ignorant people and are taken astray" (Healer Interviews 2010).

- Mainstream doctors and nurses do not fully understand traditional ways of healing and doctoring, which hampers the integration progression.

  - Mabel stresses that there is a lack of understanding and education for mainstream society. Western doctors and nurses do not really fully understand traditional ways of healing and doctoring, and this has really hampered the progression of that integration. They need to absorb themselves in cross-cultural teachings, and not be set in their ways" (Healer Interviews 2010).

  - Mabel has been involved in cross-cultural teachings for new doctors training at the medical schools. She says, "A modernized way of having the new doctors go through cross-cultural teachings will assist in the integration, and will help them in the future to start accepting more. In order for us to progress more, we need to have those resources available to have them to start working together, to work out the kinks. However, there are not enough dollars. While the health centre is doing a lot of cross-cultural teachings, the Healing Lodge is going into deficit. There is no support, and a place is needed to be able to provide the service where cross-cultural teachings can take place." Mabel questions the financial situation. She discusses a traditional healing program through Trillium that was tried. A proposal was submitted for a seven-year program to train individuals to become traditional healers in their communities. Mabel says that everyone knows that a person would not become a traditional healer in seven years (Healer Interviews 2010).

- Healers' use of poisonous plants conflicts with Western practices.

  - Mabel references poisonous plants that are used to heal. She says, "Western society would look at that and say that is a poisonous plant; you can't give them that plant. The instructions that were given to the healer were to use a poisonous plant; that is what he needed to give her to help her" (Healer Interviews 2010).

- Native people lack traditional teachings.

- Mainstream doctors frequently do not refer patients to traditional doctors.

  - The healer Francis talks about "how people are franchised for everything; they don't have teachings about that. That is the way our society wants us to be. They don't want us to use our language and traditions." Francis mentions that in the eleven years the Tribal Health Centre has existed, the Native healer has received only twenty-five referrals from the doctors in the Health Centre they are housed alongside. He says, "They just give us the ones they can't fix. The Western doctors think traditional healing is hocus pocus, witchcraft." Francis goes on to say that he thinks non-Native doctors are ignorant because they lack knowledge of traditional healing. He says ignorance can be corrected, but stupidity is forever. "A lot of people remain stupid, even in our own community" (Healer Interviews 2010).

- Healers are overworked, give up a lot personally, and are taken for granted with no consideration for their own lives or well-being.

  - Francis says, "A lot of things I give up personally to help people. I basically give my life, what other people hold important. It is so taken for granted, you know; they expect you to be there. If you are not there, they get angry. They have no consideration, you know? When my dad died, I took one day off and came out here. I was hurting from my dad being dead." People have become selfish in their pursuit of healing for their sicknesses. This becomes an issue when "the one who doctors" is overworked and sought after by insistent individuals. Francis shares a story about his mentor: "He was so busy and he never ever had a break, every day of his life for twenty years. Our trips to the First Nations would be from nine in the morning to four in the morning, and we would get up and start again till ten and eleven o'clock at night. The next day, we would drive home, and there would be four or five cars in his driveway, waiting for him when we got there. We could not even unload sometimes. They wanted to be doctored right now. No consideration ... we just traveled a fourteen-hour trip, and we just doctored for forty hours up in the bush. They have been sitting there for two dang hours waiting. That is always what I watched—the people, how they act" (Healer Interviews 2010).

- Liability insurance is needed to protect healers when they practice traditional healing methods; healers are not currently included in the First Nations' insurance clauses.

  - Lack of liability insurance to protect healers can be a deterrent to the integration of traditional and Western medicine. For example, some sweat lodge conductors are not considered to be employed by the First Nations in which they reside; they are paid honoraria (fees for service) to perform their healing, and not a wage. Other healers may be healing people from their residences (Healer Interviews 2010).

- There is a lack of belief that protection comes from the Creator as healing flows from the Creator.

- Closed minds, ignorance, and government policies interfere with integration.

  - Leonard speaks about people having closed minds, which, along with government policies, would deter the integration with Western clinics. He said, "Western health professionals just don't believe in it, and in the Western practice they just don't like waiting in line. It becomes one doctor's opinion over other things." Leonard questions why traditional healers should look for ways to integrate: "We are trying to find ways to integrate it, but they are the ones that took that out."

- Anishinaabe are not at that point of making the integration happen.

  - Leonard says that the Anishinaabe people are not really at the point of making it happen. Leonard says, "We go in and smudge people in the hospital; we go in just when they need us. When we were at the lodge, we did stuff, and they would refer people to us. It would be good to integrate. They could go in and see traditional medicine for themselves" (Healer Interviews 2010).

- People in power need to address their own health issues if they are leading others, as unhealthy people cannot lead and help others.

  - Lillie feels that the integration would be okay if the Anishinaabe people, who are in power, were on their healing path to heal from such illnesses as past trauma, sickness, or abuse. "But when the leaders are not paying attention to their own 'garbage,' they are worse than the ones that the healers are trying to heal." Lillie's helper Maggie adds, "Unhealthy people cannot help and make people healthy. Those ones that are helping others, those people that are doing traditional medicine and traditional healing need to be healthy, and in a good place, in order to help others, and sometimes that is not the case." Lillie says that "those that are walking their paths in a good way and trying to be honest, they look at you as if you are just like that other guy." She says, "Sorry, but I am not. We have too much to offer each other, once we get rid of the ego, and power and control, it will be so. I tell them to leave their ego at home" (Healer Interviews 2010).

- Healers need to be healthy in order to help others.

- Mainstream societies need to acquire diplomas through academic life and work life, and older traditional healers prefer not to attend school.

  - Bill calls the diploma the biggest barrier. He says, "The fact is that in Western medicine you have to go to school, you have to work, and you have to have the diploma. The biggest barrier is that they want you to go back to school. A lot of people are fifty to sixty years old. You know they don't want to go back to school. I have a brother that makes medicine; he does not want to go back to school." Bill reflects on the way reserves are set up where there are a lot of them that are split. "Families are different, families do this, and different families do that, and churches still play a big part in First Nations people's lives, the religion part of it" (Healer Interviews 2010).

- Traditional medicine cannot be mass produced, cannot be patented, as patenting traditional medicine will not work in combining traditional and Western practices.
  - Bill reflects on the fact that "you cannot mass produce traditional medicine." Mabel mentions that medicine cannot be patented. Mabel says we need "hands-on research to find cures with natural medicine but no patent on the medicine, as it would be destructive and not work between the traditional and Western practices" (Healer Interviews 2010).
- People continue to practice in secrecy.

Mabel says, "I think a lot of people are in the secrecy stage. I suggest educating people to become self-sustaining within their family regarding healthcare. In the past, there was a tribal way of living and everyone contributed. Everyone is gifted in a different way, so how can we move forward if people keep it a secret? Colonialism said, 'Here is a priest, and only the priest has a relationship with the Creator.' In our beliefs, everyone has a relationship with the Creator. Certain people say that they can only be a doctor. Our people can all do doctoring, and do doctoring work because we have that gift to be able to do that." Francis who is a medicine man talks about only certain people having the gift to heal - 'God-given natural born ability, natural spirit ability, not everybody can heal' (Healer Interviews 2010).

- Pharmacies and doctors have shares in pharmaceutical companies. Big industries want money and keep society trapped.

Clients of Healers' Perspectives

Clients of healers perceive very similar barriers to those mentioned by healers to the integration of traditional and Western practices. They include:

- Western medicine does not understand the holistic part of traditional healing; it only addresses the physical.
  - Hope mentions that she "would see the traditional and Western medicines as separate services, but working cooperatively for the overall health, for whomever. Western medicine does

not understand the holistic part of traditional healing. They only address the physical, and there is a fear that there is no understanding of what traditional healing really is. You can take workshops and you can go to seminars, but you really don't know what it is like unless you are Anishinaabe" (Client Interview 2010).

- There are attitudes and battles between pharmacists and doctors.

  - Francine and John, a couple who visits the healer Tom, think that the integration of traditional and Western medicine will not happen because of the friction between the two and the attitudes that fester between doctors and pharmacists. "There is a big battle there" (Client Interviews 2010).

- Western doctors do not believe in traditional healing medicine or practices.

  - Francine and John say that Western doctors do not believe in traditional healing. They comment that most doctors do not know about it, and don't believe in it. They do not discuss traditional medicine with their doctors.

- New learners are not as experienced with traditional medicine and healing.

  - Francine and John continue, "It depends on the people that you teach traditional medicine to; a person like Tom, he already knows what to do, where some are just learning" (Client Interviews 2010).

- Not many people know about traditional healers.

  - Both Francine and John have found that when they asked people in the community about healers, nobody knew about them; they found Tom on their own. John says, "Tom needs help now that he is getting older" (Client Interviews 2010).

- There is a lack of trust; once Native people visit a traditional healer, some refrain from visiting Western doctors.

  - Jean says, "No trust, lack of trust, I would think. Some of our people won't see a Western doctor once they have seen what our healers can do. They just will say that is enough of that, why should I put all of those chemicals in my body when I can take all of this natural medicine? I can go to ceremonies,

I can go to sweat lodges, I can fast to get my answers. For whatever they are going through and for whatever reason, whether it is mental health, or emotional, or something like, you know, there are things that you can do like sweat lodges, ceremonies, fasting, and there is medicine out there for that. There is lavender to calm you down. There are all kinds of medicines to help you take care of yourself" (Client Interviews 2010).

- Healers are overworked; another venue is required in order to meet the demand.

  - Hope thinks that it would be a good idea to integrate. She says, "I know even the neighboring reserves, and even one of the other organizations has someone come in, and they are just swamped; if there was another venue for people to go to, they would go" (Client Interviews 2010).

Summary of Findings and Recommendations

The problems and solutions that are discovered from this study on "Integrating Traditional Medicine and Healers into Western Clinics" emerge from the voices of the research participants—the health director, the health professionals, the healers, and the clients of healers. The ultimate goal of this project is to better serve and provide choices for First Nations peoples to access traditional holistic healing at Western clinics.

Following are key points regarding health problems, barriers to integration, and appropriate names for healers, and recommendations for pursuing integrated health systems and working toward a traditional, holistic environment within Western clinics. A traditional and Western integration can be a means of assisting in the health and well-being of all people.

Major health problems facing Native people

- Diabetes

- Addictions

- Mental Health

- Cancer

- Heart Disease/Problems

Barriers to the integration of traditional medicine/healers with Western clinics

- Lack of knowledge and understanding of traditional healing methods

- Lack of knowledge of aboriginal culture and issues
- Lack of funding provided by Health Canada
- Lack of exposure to traditional healers and medicine
- Lack of knowledge about traditional healers
- Fear of the unknown
- Conditioning can cause fear
- Influences of Christianity
- Impact from Residential Schools, including loss of language, culture, and traditions
- Family loss of cultural teachings because of parents being raised in Residential Schools
- Fewer opportunities to draw healers, to find healing, and to receive answers from traditional ceremonies with sacred fires
- Large geographical distances with no transportation
- Preferred healer from the United States
- Overworked healers taken for granted
- Lack of knowledge and acceptance by health professionals
- Western medicine not understanding or believing in the holistic part of traditional healing
- Lack of referrals by Western practitioners to traditional healers
- Reluctance to be seen as "quack" by their Western colleagues
- Mainstream society's need to acquire diplomas (academic life and work life)
- Older traditional healers preferring not to attend school
- New learners with not as much experience with traditional medicine and healing
- Lack of cross-cultural teachings
- Conflict with Western practices, with healers' use of poisonous plants
- Inability to mass produce or patent traditional medicine
- Lack of appropriate space
- Lack of funding and deficits preventing traditional healing lodge use

- Lack of funding and cutbacks preventing traditional healers from healing people
- Christian stigma toward traditional healers
- Lack of interest by community members
- Lack of trust in Western doctors once they visit traditional healers
- Ignorance and closed minds
- Lack of readiness for integration
- Inadequate knowledge available for seekers of traditional healers
- Lack of opportunity to learn about traditional healing
- Lack of training and certification
- Lack of consistency in training of healers
- Lack of process in how to integrate traditional healing into Western practices
- Lack of planning
- Lack of identification of aboriginal clients within Western practices
- Lack of authentic traditional healers
- Secrecy
- Colonialism's control and limiting of traditional beliefs
- Disbelief
- Traditional healing's effect on Western practices as people access healers
- Non-Native people practicing Anishinaabe healing ceremonies
- Experience of "Bad Medicine"
- Lack of liability insurance to protect healers
- Pharmaceutical companies keeping society trapped
- Attitudes and battles between pharmacists and doctors
- Disbelief that protection comes from the Creator
- Inability of unhealthy people to lead and help others
- Inability of unhealthy healers to help others

- Government standards, safety concerns from pharmaceutical companies

Appropriate names for healers in the Anishinaabe culture

- The one who doctors—*naan dawi ji ge-(nini)*
- Medicine Man, Medicine Woman, or Medicine Person/People
- Traditional Healer
- Helper to the Creator
- The Healer
- Traditional Medicine Person
- Gifted with the plants
- Traditional Doctor

Recommendations
Increasing access to traditional healers

- Design "An Integrated Planning Process" by First Nations
- Identify healers and determine the Anishinaabe name for healer
- Utilize the knowledge and experience of traditional healers
- Teach healers, health professionals (Native and non-Native), and community members about traditional medicine and healing, and the Anishinaabe tradition and culture
- Provide a choice in healing systems (traditional and Western)
- Plan a pay scale for healers equal to Western practices
- Health Canada policies need to be led by Anishinaabe people

Integrating Traditional Healing and Western Medicine

The integration of traditional medicine and healers into Western health clinics can be made possible by providing the tools necessary to complete the tasks to incorporate and provide better ways in which to heal the people. Following are ideas and suggestions made by the participants of the research project:

- Increase education regarding traditional culture and healing among Anishinaabe people and Western medical professionals

- Fund traditional healers on a regular basis
- Cover the cost of the medicine chest to support traditional healers in doing the healing work
- Use traditional medicine intravenously to accelerate the recovery process and heal
- Institute a combined system (doctor and healer work side by side)
- Combine health forms and records
- Share medical information
- Compromise for conditions (i.e., hospitals—smudge, drum, sing)
- Take the burden off the health care system; pay out because it will cut costs down the road
- Work together to be able to do hands-on research in finding cures with natural medicines and chart the well-being of people
- Use the medicinal testing apparatus for medicine interactions of Western and traditional medicines
- Research and Analyze
- Note the benefit of having no chemicals in natural medicines
- Create policies and procedures for traditional medicine and healers and Western practices
- Let the healer and the helper work together
- Work together with patient (doctor and healer) to see how the medicine will work
- Use tobacco (simaa), as it is the traditional contract between the client and the healer
- Allow Western doctors to diagnose and refer to traditional healers—and vice versa
- Respect choice of traditional or Western medicines
- Incorporate a "Parallel System" of mutual respect and referrals from one to the other

Cultural and Healing Education
- Offer community awareness workshops by healers

- Teach traditional healing methods
- Experience the traditional healing
- Produce newsletters and teach aboriginal youth
- Provide cross-cultural teachings for physicians and Health Canada
- Create a learning environment for cultural teachings
- Design professional learning manuals
- Development of an Apprenticeship Program
- Create one-year cross-cultural internships for Western and traditional practitioners (let Western practitioners intern with traditional and vice versa)
- Develop workshops on eating, harvesting, and purchasing natural foods—a Native diet
- Organic gardening and access to safer water
- Educate on the Vision of the Integration process

Political

- Research, investigate and collaborate with the existing Aboriginal political bodies that have worked to integrate traditional and Western practices, such as the First Nations Leadership Council of British Columbia; the Mi'kmaq of Nova Scotia; the Council of Yukon Indians of Whitehorse, Yukon, Canada; Wikwemikong First Nation of Manitoulin Island, Ontario; the Sault Tribe of Chippewa, Sault Sainte Marie, Michigan; and the World Health Organization (WHO).

- Work collaboratively with these organizations to design an "Integrated Planning Process by First Nations" to integrate traditional medicine and healers into Western clinics, in order to ensure the revival of the Anishinaabe culture and traditions and to improve the health of Aboriginal peoples. Through these processes, the sensitivity of patenting traditional medicines is of a critical concern.

- Form a Council of Traditional Medicine People across the North Shore area, inviting other communities to integrate into a First Nations Council for a Traditional Health Care System.

Personal Reflections on Practicum
Limitations and Challenges

The major challenges of the research study were:

- Travel to conduct research with the NSTCHC and healers outside the local area

- Reluctance of some individuals to fill out client surveys

- Difficulties with some individual responses to requests that required leadership contact

- Native organizations require individual connections with autonomous leadership

- The extra effort needed to participate in the research project added to workers' responsibilities

The major limitations of this research study were:

- Limited client surveys at some First Nations; there were difficulties finding participants

- Limited interest in traditional medicine/healers from some organizations

- Limited knowledge of traditional medicine/healer use in the communities

Support for the research project includes:

- Proven track record from the responses made by all participants

- Interest was shown by the director, professionals, healers, clients

- The need to support the initiative was agreed upon throughout the research

The research project was overall a great experience that has helped me to gain knowledge of the health practices administered by Western practitioners and traditional healers, and of their clients. My knowledge and understanding of "Integrating Traditional Medicine and Healers into Western Clinics" has increased through the anthropological research that was conducted with the peoples of the NSTCHC, the First Nations, and the Indian Friendship Centre.

Globally, nationally, locally, and politically, I have gained scholarly knowledge and understanding of the barriers to the "Integration of Traditional Medicine and Healers into Western clinics." I have grown to understand the political restraints and broken promises of the political leadership in Canada, and the historical and contemporary Native leadership's struggles for solidarity for First Nations peoples.

Nationally and provincially, I have gained knowledge of how First Nations peoples work toward the integration process, trying to overcome the barriers, in which to heal the people from historical trauma and health issues that face indigenous peoples today. The participants' experiential input has helped me to interpret the culture and traditions of the Anishinaabe people through the healers who heal, the clients who feel better, the administration, and the political leaders who either support or are so far removed from the Anishinaabe cultural ways of healing that they do not set traditional healing as a high priority for their health centres. The health centres that do integrate are supporting their traditional ways of life by giving wholeheartedly, holistically, and spiritually, and by fulfilling their call in life from the Creator. They have been gifted as "helpers of the Creator," as the "the one who doctors," or as the "medicine people," but this position of "healer" is not always authentic. The authentic "healers" are those that carry the gifts to heal.

Globally, I have gained insight into the WHO's perspective and support of TM/CAM (Traditional Medicine/Complementary and Alternative Medicine). I have gained insight into how traditional medicine is similar to that found in other cultures and traditions across the globe; leaders in traditional medicine continue their great effort to find ways to address the same types of concerns indigenous peoples struggle with around the world, when they try to keep ancient medicine and modalities of healing sacred, useful, and at the forefront of their nations.

Anthropology has contributed to the project on "Integrating Traditional Medicine and Healers into Western Clinics." An initiative and an ethnographic approach became a researchable project when I used the data and analyzed qualitative and quantitative information collected from contributors and participant observations. The outcome of the anthropological research brings meaning and knowledge to both indigenous and nonindigenous peoples. The research project helps me to better understand and clarify injustices, health practices, integration processes, and holistic views on ancient ways of healing. The participants have genuinely provided a script in which to continue from this initial research project that provided the data collection, study and analysis, and the many findings and recommendations that may be administratively or politically taken to the next step in "Integrating Traditional Medicine and Healers into Western Clinics." A stepping-stone approach to the restoration and revitalization of the Anishinaabe culture and traditions that are carved in the traditional medicines and modalities of healing is realistic.

Glossary

clans: Animal totems (dodems).

COPD: Chronic Obstructive Pulmonary Disease.

minigan: Medicinal salve made from black poplar buds and other ingredients to heal.

Medicine Wheel: The Anishinaabe or Ojibwa nation has a teaching that the Medicine Wheel is the circle of life. All of creation is represented on the Medicine Wheel. The Medicine Wheel also includes all nations on Earth, not just the Ojibwa people. The teaching is that all things in life are in a circle. The earth is a circle or sphere as are the sun, the moon, and all of the other planets and stars in our universe. The cycles of the seasons and day and night are circular. The life cycle is circular from birth to childhood to youth to adulthood to old age and finally to death and rebirth. These teachings are divided into the four directions—East, South, West, and North.

OECD: Organization for Economic Co-operation and Development.

simaa: Ojibwe word for tobacco, one of the four sacred plants.

Bibliography

Assembly of First Nations. Retrieved October 30, 2010 from http://www.afn. ca/cmslib/general/afn_rcap.pdf.

Beaver, Jan. "Medicine Wheel," 2009. Retrieved from http://osee.jamescreech. com/conferences/2009/Medicine_Wheel_Direction

Biolsi, Thomas, ed. *A Companion to the Anthropology of American Indians.* New York: Wiley, 2005.

Broome, Barbara and Rochelle Broome. "Native Americans: Traditional Healing." *Urological Nursing* 27:2. University of South Alabama College of Nursing, April 2007.

Brown, Patricia Leigh. "A Doctor for Disease, A Shaman for the Soul." *New York Times,* Sept. 19, 2009. Retrieved from http://www.nytimes.com/2009/09/20/ us/20shaman.html?_r=2&em=&adxnnl=1&adxnnlx=1253578564-HaXhrN8vjA51Zs72mBiySg

Cook, Jane Sarah. "Use of traditional Mi'kmaq medicine among patients at a First Nations Community Health Centre: Dalhousie Medical School Department of Family Medicine Rural Summer Program." *Journal of Society of Rural Physicians of Canada*, 2009: 1–5. Retrieved from www. cma.ca/index.cfm/ci_id/43592/la_id/1.htm.

"Evidence-based Complementary and Alternative Medicine." *Oxford Journal* 7:3–4, June and Sept. 2010.

Frideres, James, S. "The Royal Commission on Aboriginal Peoples: The Route to Self-Government?" Department of Sociology, the University of CalGabriel, CalGabriel, Alberta, Canada. Retrieved October 30, 2010 from http://www2.brandonu.ca/library/cjns/16.2/frideres.pdf

Harris, Samela. "Medicine Men." *The Advertiser*, August 13, 2009: 1–3.

Health Canada.

Health Care System. First Ministers' Meeting with Leaders of National Aboriginal Organizations, November 24-25, 2005. http://www.hc-sc.

gc.ca/hcs-sss/delivery-prestation/fptcollab/2005-fmm-rpm-abor-auto/ index-eng.php. Accessed October 30, 2010.

Health Canada. Indian and Northern Affairs Canada.

Federal Ministers and National Aboriginal Leaders Participate in Joint Policy Retreat. Ottawa, Ontario (May 31, 2005). http://www.ainc-inac.gc.ca/ai/ mr/nr/m-a2005/2-02665-eng.asp. Accessed October 30, 2010.

Health Canada. First Nations Inuit Health

Lemchuk-Favel, Laurel. FAV COM Financing a First Nations & Inuit Integrated Health System: A Discussion Document [Health Canada], 1999. http:// www.hc-sc.gc.ca/fniah-spnia/pubs/finance/_agree-ccord/1999_finance_ integr/index-eng.php Accessed October 30, 2010.

Health Canada. Statistics Canada http://www.statcan.gc.ca/stcsr/query.html? btn=Tablesandqt=First+Nations+in+O. Accessed November 13, 2010.

Jacklin, Kristen. "Diversity within: Deconstructing Aboriginal community health in Wikwemikong Unceded Indian Reserve." *Social Science and Medicine.* Northern Ontario School of Medicine and Human Sciences. Sudbury, Ontario. Canada: Elsevier Ltd., 2008. 980–989.

Jacklin, Kristen and Wayne, Warry "The Indian Health Transfer Policy in Canada: Toward Self-Determination or Cost Containment?" *Unhealthy Health Policy: A Critical Anthropological Examination*, ed. Arachu Castro and Merrill Singer. Walnut Creek, CA: Altamira Press, 2008. 215–233.

Jones N.P., J.T. Arnason, M. Abou-Zaid, K. Akpagana, P Sanchez-Vindas, and M.L. Smith ML. "Antifungal Activity of Extracts from Medicinal Plants used by First Nations Peoples of Eastern Canada." *Journal of Ethnopharmacology.* 73. 191–198.

Jorge, Rome "The plant whisperer: Philippine herbal medicine pioneer Nelia Maramba, MD." *Manila Times,* July 26, 2009. 1–3.

"Reports from S.B. Kosalge et al. Highlight Research in Ethnopharmaceutical." *Drug Week.* April 22, 2009 Retrieved from http://goliath.ecnext.com/ coms2/gi_0199-10431472/Reports-from-S-B-Kosalge.html.

Mamaweswen. Annual Report 2009-2010. Retrieved October 21, 2010 from http://www.mamaweswen.ca/administration/ar2010.pdf.

McCoy Brian F. "Outside the Ward and Clinic, Healing the Aboriginal Body." Australian Research Centre in Sex, Health, and Society (ARCSHS), 2008. La Trobe University, Australia. 226–245.

McGee Jon R. and Warms, Richard L. 2008. *Anthropological Theory. An Introductory History.* New York: McGraw-Hill, 2008.

Medicine, Beatrice. *Learning to Be an Anthropologist and Remaining "Native."* Champaign, IL: University of Illinois Press, 2001.

"Medterms." Retrieved December 6, 2010. http://www.medterms.com/script/main/art.asp?articlekey=33979.

National Center for Complementary and Alternative Medicine. 2010. Retrieved December 3, 2010. http://nccam.nih.gov/health/what is cam/.

Osman, Salim "Child 'healer' sparks debate: *The Straits Times*, March 20, 2009. 1–2.

Parlee, Brenda, John O'Neil and Lutsel K'e Dene First Nation.2007. "The Dene Way of Life: Perspectives on Health from Canada's North." *Journal of Canadian Studies,* 41:3, Fall 2007. 112–133.

Ramsey, Doug and Kenneth Beesley, "Rural Community Well-being: The Perspectives of Health Care Managers in Southwestern Manitoba, Canada." *Journal of Rural and Community Development,* 2006. 86–107.

Robson, Robert. "Suffering an Excessive Burden: Housing as a Health Determinant in The First Nations Community of Northwestern Ontario." *The Canadian Journal of Native Studies* 28:1. 71–87.

Rosenberg, Mark W. and Wilson, Kathleen. "Exploring the Determinants of Health for First Nations Peoples in Canada: Can Existing Frameworks Accommodate Traditional Activities?" *Social Science and Medicine* 55, McMaster University. 2017–31.

Sommers, Elizabeth, Ahmad al-Hadidi, and Kristin Porter. "International Efforts toward Integrated Care: Acupuncture in Iraq." *The American Acupuncturist*, Summer 2009. 36–37.

Steeves, Dale and Marisa Adair. "B.C. Launches First-Ever First Nations Health Plan."Office of the Premier, Ministry of Health, First Nations Leadership Council. November 27, 2006. Retrieved from http://www.gov.bc.ca/arr/social/health/plan.html; http://www.mediaroom.gov.bc.ca/video/Health_MO.

Summary of the Final Report of the Royal Commission on Aboriginal Peoples: Implications for Canada's Health Care System. Institute on Governance. Ottawa, Ontario, Canada, 2009.

Tidemand, Adolph. "Legal Herbs. from Remedies and Rituals." *The American Herb Association* 24:4, 2009. 6.

"Urban Myth? Evidence-Based Medicine." New Zealand Press Association, October 18, 2009. 1–7.

Wheatley, Margaret A. "Developing an Integrated Traditional/Clinical Health System in the Yukon." *Circumpolar Health* 90, 1990. 217–220.

WHO Report. World Health Organization, 2010. Retrieved from http://www.who.int/medicines/areas/traditional/en/index.html; http://www.who.int/topics/traditional_medicine/en/.

Appendix A

Along the North shore
The First Nations' Communities'
Traditional lodges and Western clinics
Places of prayer – Traditional and Christian

Figure 1 Garden River Wellness Centre (Western)

Figure 2 Traditional Healing Lodge
Garden River First Nation, Garden River, Ontario Canada

Figure 3 North Shore Tribal Council Administration
Buildings, Cutler, Ontario

Figure 4 Sault Ste. Marie Indian Friendship Centre

Figure 5 Batchewana First Nation Health Centre
(Rankin) (no traditional healing lodge)

Figure 6 Serpent River First Nation Health Centre

Figure 7 Traditional Lodge at Serpent River First
Nation (located on the Healer's land)

Figure 8 At Blind River near Mississauga First Nation
Anishnabie Naadmaagi Gamig Substance Abuse Treatment Centre

Figure 9 Blessed Kateri Parish (Closed)
the welcome sign outside Blessed Kateri Parish at Mississauga First Nation

Figure 10 Traditional Healing Lodge at Thessalon First Nation

Figure 11 Sweat Lodge at Garden River First Nation

Appendix B

Appendix C

WHEN THE PAST MEETS THE PRESENT

Figure 12 "Misshepezhieu" Agawa Indian Pictographs at Lake Superior in
Ontario – Our past is our present in the Ojibwe Culture,
The Misshepezhieu (water spirit) is seen by seers of the Ojibwe people today

Figure 13 Agawa Indian Pictographs, Lake Superior - Ontario

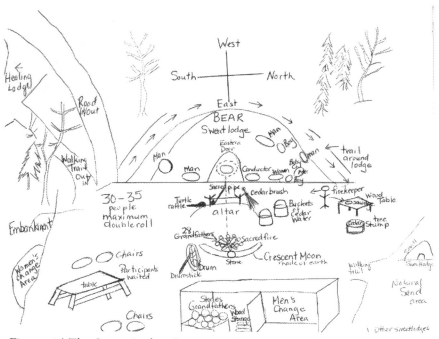

Figure 14 The Sweat Lodge Ceremony Participant Observation Diagram

Figure 15 Sandhill Cranes (Chieftainship, Leadership Clan)

Figure 16 The Clans (Totems), The Bear (Healer, Policing of the People)

My gratitude to the Creator for the guidance and
blessings I receive on my spiritual journey.

Chi-Miigwetch – Thank you